Edible
LANDSCAPING
WITH A PERMACULTURE TWIST

HOW TO HAVE YOUR YARD AND EAT IT TOO

MICHAEL JUDD

Photo Credits:
The images in this book were taken from Michael Judd's iPhone, except for the following:
© Michael McConkey: Front cover fruit banner, 72, 74, 77 (top), 82, 83; (c) Laurel Silvio: Back cover (top right); © Scott Keimig: 16 (bottom); © Field & Forest Products: 49 (top); © Raintree Nursery: 90; © Tom Ditmars, NJ Food Forest: 107; © Harvey Ussery: 109; © Alicia Moulton, Boozed + Infused: 114; © Steve Hesselink: 131.

ISBN: 978-0-615-87379-4

Edited by Wendi Hoover and Nicole Robinson
Book design by Ponderosa Pine Design, Vicky Vaughn Shea

Illustrations by:
Matthew VonHerbulis
Creative Services
www.MatthewVonHerbulis.com

Distributed in the U.S. by Chelsea Green Publishing

Printed in Hong Kong by Regent Publishing Services Ltd.
Printed with vegetable-based inks and FSC certified paper. FSC, Forest Stewardship Council, is an international certification organization that assures their products meet forest management standards that expand protection of water quality, prohibit harvest of rare old-growth forest, prevent loss of natural forest cover and prohibit highly hazardous chemicals.

Disclaimer: Information in this book is based on hands-on experience. The author is not a trained professional in any health, environmental, or other field; he will not be responsible for the consequences of the application of any information or ideas presented herein.

This book is dedicated to my folks, Chris and Carolyn Judd, who have always supported my wild adventures with faith.

Table of Contents

Introduction

EDIBLE LANDSCAPING IS THE NEW AMERICAN GARDEN

It cross-pollinates a desire for tasty food with nostalgia, greater food security, and a need to stop mowing so damn much.

At heart edible landscaping is about re-enlivening the adventure of creating useful landscapes. Gardening is meant to be fun but can quickly wear thin when there is a lack of design to support healthy plants. "Edible Landscaping with a Permaculture Twist" digs right into simple designs that focus on how to begin and end projects that set the stage for successful growing and unique looking landscapes.

You will find the pages of this book filled with actual designs I have created and built over years of workshops, homesteading and running an edible landscaping business. Though geared toward suburbia and starting from scratch, the designs can be easily grafted to the micro-habits of the urban landscape, scaled up to the acreage of homesteads, or adapted to already flourishing landscapes. It's a tool to wield as your imagination feels fit.

The chapters' step-by-step approaches to projects require only your will and interest to begin flipping your yard into an edible oasis. You'll discover the ease and fun of building herb spirals, growing fantastic-tasting mushrooms, designing a garden that waters itself, shaping up an earthen oven, selecting and planting funky fruits, turning your harvests into booze, establishing a food forest, and so much more.

It's a book to be carried out into the landscape, propped open with a rock, dog-eared, penciled in, smudged with dirty fingers, and pelted by the occasional rain.

So don't you dare leave it on the coffee table. It's going help you carve your little piece of suburbia into something luscious and productive.

The Permaculture Twist

Permaculture is a holistic landscape design practice coined and introduced in the late 1970s by wild Tasmanian woodsman, Bill Mollison, and his student, David Holmgren. By taking indigenous knowledge, the observation of natural patterns, and applying modern realities, these two cooked up a fantastic set of design principals and ethics that guide practitioners in designing self-sustaining, abundant landscapes.

Good permaculture design brings all the elements in your landscape together to create a

Permaculture combines gardening, natural building, forestry, animal husbandry, alternative technology, social dynamics, economics, and much more into a holistic design for human habitats. (Image courtesy Karl J. Schmidt/Glacial Lakes Permaculture)

FOOD · SHELTER · ENERGY · ETHICS · CLIMATE · WATER · SOIL

PERMACULTURE

A design system for ecological and sustainable living, integrating plants, animals, buildings, people, and communities.

harmonious whole. Each aspect of the landscape is placed where it relates to the whole and flow. Parts of the design are not thought of separately but designed together to support each other. In keeping with that principle, the chapters of this book are woven together where possible to help you create thriving landscapes that function for themselves—a.k.a., less time with your mower and more time in the hammock.

Permaculture principles can be put to work in the smallest urban space or on spacious farms and in entire watersheds. They are adaptable to every site, based on your goals and the elements present. Many of the designs I highlight in the book are born of permaculture design and inspiring examples I have seen by fellow practitioners in all kinds of spaces. The basic design patterns I provide are flexible, allowing you to add your own twists and create the balance that suits your homescape.

The trick is just jumping in, going for it, and observing what works and flows. And above all . . .

. . . remember to have a good time!

— Aryeh Elliott and Emmet Agoston at Mt. View Farm's earthen oven workshop, 2011

Herb Spiral
THE ULTIMATE RAISED BED

Benefits

There are many benefits to planting an herb spiral raised bed garden:

- Fantastic year-round edible landscape architecture
- Creates micro-climates for your favorite herbs and veggies
- Easy and fun to build
- Space and water saver
- High productivity in a small space
- Can fit anywhere, even on patios

Why the Spiral?

The garden spiral is like a snail shell, with stone spiraling upward to create multiple micro-climates and a cornucopia of flavors on a small footprint. Spirals can come in any size to fit any space, from an urban courtyard to an entire yard. You don't even need a patch of ground, as they can be built on top of patios, pavement, and rooftops. You can spiral over an old stump or on top of poor soil. By building up vertically, you create more growing space, make watering easy, and lessen the need to bend over while harvesting. To boot, spirals add instant architecture and year-round beauty to your landscape: the perfect garden focal point.

One of the beauties of an herb spiral is that you are creating multiple micro-climates in a small space. The combination of stones, shape, and vertical structure offers a variety of planting niches for a diversity of plants. The stones also serve as a thermal mass, minimizing temperature swings and extending the growing seasons. Whatever you grow in your spiral, it will pump out a great harvest for the small space it occupies. I've grown monstrous cucumbers in my large garden spiral, with one plant producing over 30 prize-size fruits. The spiral is a food-producing superstar!

Habitat

Stacked stones create perennial habitat for beneficial critters, such as lizards and spiders that help balance pest populations in the garden. The stone network is a year-round safe haven for beneficial insects and other crawlies that work constantly to keep your garden in balance—and you in the hammock. A little design for them up-front pays big, tasty dividends later.

Spiral Construction

There are two basic approaches to building a spiral: dry stack and free form.

Dry Stack

Materials for a Dry Stack Spiral, Six-Foot Diameter

- ❑ 90 granite blocks
- ❑ Cardboard
- ❑ 1 cubic yard soil/compost mix

Dry stacking refers to a free-standing structure of stone carefully placed to hold form without concrete. Dry stacking the rock has the advantage of the spiral staying put (not shifting), allowing you to create an herb spiral in a tight or formal setting. Cut granite blocks work well for dry stacking when the spiral has a diameter of five feet or more. An alternative to granite block is any kind of stackable stone, such as slate flagstone, cut wall stone, or even brick, which can help shape a smaller diameter spiral.

This small dry stack spiral is approximately three-and-a-half feet wide by two feet high.

LAY IT DOWN, DRY-STACK STYLE

Lay down cardboard in an area one foot larger than the diameter of the intended finished spiral. Cardboard kills grass under the spiral, helps prevent weeds from growing around the spiral's edge, and creates a ring for mulch when you're done creating your spiral.

You can start by drawing a spiral on the cardboard, or you can simply begin laying out the first layer of block in the shape you're after. Be sure the spacing allows for the final planting bed width, which needs to be at least 8 inches wide. Ideally, the lowest point faces north and the spiral builds clockwise. While this layout and direction is helpful, it is not essential. I often choose my starting point based on the site and aesthetics. The design in the picture series here is approximately six feet in diameter by three feet high. Every two-and-a-half blocks, begin the next layer known as a 'course' in masonry terms for at least four courses, to gain your eventual height. This stepping up is easily understood once you start laying the stone.

Dry stack layout

Dry stack winding up.

Fill bottom with gravel or wood chips, then top off with soil/compost mix.

Viola! Dry stack ready to plant.

Since we are making a round spiral out of square blocks, the innermost part of the spiral gets tight and a little tricky. I use broken bits of block, pieces of brick, and whatever else I can get my hands on to recycle and reuse, making the innermost turns. Visually, it doesn't matter because it will not be seen in the end. For the final twist at the top, I like to end it off with a few hand-picked quartz stones or whatever small colorful stone I can find. The finished dry stack may still be a little wobbly. To add more support, I fill the bottom of the herb spiral's center with gravel or wood chips; this also helps with drainage and prevents water from collecting and heaving when frozen. Then, I either make or order a soil mix that is about 40% compost to 60% soil and fill it the rest of the way to the top of the spiral. If any blocks are loose or leaning outward, I tuck them in toward the soil. And, voila! Your herb spiral is ready to plant.

Do not worry if you don't get a perfect spiral or rounded curves; most imperfections are lost in the overall charm and uniqueness of your spiral. Surprisingly, soil does not come flushing out the cracks, and the little that does makes a good rockery planting.

Note: You can cap the bottom with a cross-set stone or just let it flow out into a surrounding garden. Another option for the bottom end is to put in a little frog pond or depression; a neat way to do this is to bury a metal bucket so the lip is flush with the ground and fill it with water.

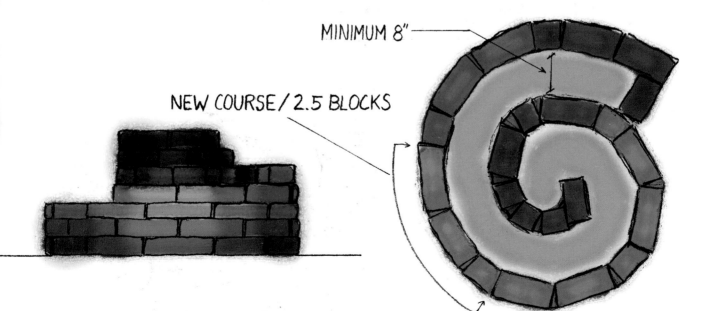

MINIMUM 8"

NEW COURSE / 2.5 BLOCKS

Free Form

Materials for a Free Form Spiral, Eight-Foot Diameter

- ❑ 1 pallet of wall stone (1.5 ton)
- ❑ Cardboard
- ❑ 4 cubic yards soil/compost mix

The easiest way to build a spiral is the free form way. Simply create a mound of mixed soil and compost (60% soil, 40% compost), shape it into a spiral, and fit the stones into the spiral. The downside to this design is that the structure can shift as soil settles and freezes. But it uses less stone and offers flexibility in the type of stone used, such as round field stone. Free form spirals lend themselves to larger spirals that can easily cover more than 12 feet and can be planted with heat-loving veggies, such as peppers, cucumbers, and tomatoes, which will produce prolifically. With all that loose soil and balanced temperature from the rocks, the veggies will love it!

Free form shaping and stone placing.

Shaping the free form spiral.

Robert Strasser stacking it up with Chulo Dog guarding.

Free form spiral sittin' pretty.

Free form spirals can be really big—even big enough to walk right into them. Or they can be compact enough to fit into the garden. If you go big, just plan to place in stepping-stones on the beds to reach the center; or if you go really big, make a walking path up the bed. An advantage of free form stone stacking is that you can lean the stones into the soil, which supports them easily without a perfect dry stack balance and allows a broader range of stones to be used, like the funky found stone design shown on page 17.

Note: I tend to make my free forms tall in expectation of some sinking; for any designs five feet or larger in diameter, plan at least three feet in height.

The spiral picture series here was built as a centerpiece to a butterfly meadow and measures approximately 12 feet in diameter by three feet in height. Six yards of premixed soil and compost were dumped right on site. Chocolate Grey Stone, one-and-a-third pallets weighing approximately 4,000 pounds, were also dropped right on site. If you cannot get materials dropped right on the site, try to get them as close as possible, or you're going to be doing a lot of wheelbarrowing, which is still well worth the spiral gem you'll have when done. Likewise, you can hand-mix the top soil/compost and use whatever stone you may have laying around.

After laying down cardboard and taking bed width into consideration, I begin "ramping" the soil at the chosen low-end point, rising slowly up as I round the pile. For the butterfly meadow spiral, the planting bed width is approximately 20 inches wide; for smaller designs, only go as narrow as eight inches. Have fun until you are happy with the spiral

Free form with found stone.

shape and bed width. Then, walk along the inside of the spiral, compacting where the stone will be laid. Also, feel free to leave the spiral to sit and settle for a few days.

Spread out your stones so you can pick and choose the right one for each spot. This is where those kindergarten puzzle-making skills finally come to fruition. The shape you raked out will dictate where and how high the stones need to be. The stones will lean in and onto the shaped spiral, offering support, which makes stacking a breeze. Start at the top or bottom and spiral down or up.

Planting the Spiral, Filling the Niches

Exposed to the sun and wind, the top of the spiral is great for crowning with Mediterranean herbs, such as rosemary, thyme, and oregano. Coming down the spiral as it faces east and the morning light, we find a good place for more delicate plants, such as parsley and chives. Then around the sunny south and west sides, basil, lavender, and sages will do great. At the low, moist, north-facing side, cilantro and cress will thrive. To maximize the micro-climates, design the low side of the spiral end to face north.

With such a variety of niches, the spirals can be planted with just about anything. It does not have to be for only growing herbs or reserved for areas with lots of sun. Simply maximize on your location and plant interests.

Considerations

Do keep in mind that with all the stone and raised height, the spiral can dry out faster than a traditional ground-based garden. The smaller dry stack designs tend to dry out easily, given the soil-to-stone ratio. The larger free form spirals are basically a huge pile of soil and will retain more moisture. If worried about the spiral drying out, just focus on planting Mediterranean herbs, which can take the drought, no problem. In winter, I just mulch over the beds or let the herbs perennialize. Either way, it keeps an attractive visual interest in your landscape through all the seasons.

Don't feel a need for rock skill or perfection, no two spirals are alike! Just jump in, stack it up, plant, harvest, and enjoy!

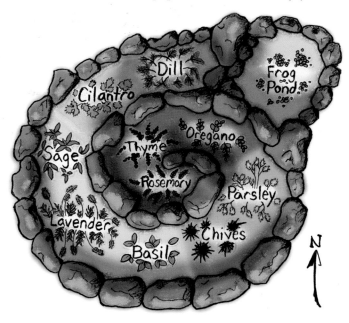

MEDITERRANEAN TOP
Windy and Sunny
Susceptible to drying out
Great for mediterraneans

DELICATE EAST
Exposed to gentle morning sun
Ideal for delicate plants

SUNNY SOUTHWEST
A great home for your Sun-lovers

LOW NORTH
For shade and moisture prefering plants
A great opportunity to flow your spiral into a small pond.

Raspberry Thyme Tom Collins

INGREDIENTS - MAKES 1 DRINK

- ⅓ cup raspberries
- 2 sprigs of thyme
- ¼ cup good dry gin
- 3 tsb sugar
- ¼ cup water
- Juice of one lemon
- Tonic to taste

PUT IT TOGETHER

Heat the sugar and lemon in water, stirring constantly until the sugar has dissolved. Allow to cool.

Remove the thyme leaves from the stems and mash together with the raspberries. Save a few leaves and berries whole to garnish later.

Stir together the mash and sugared water while still warm. Cool to room temperature.

Shake the mixture with the gin, pour over ice, and add tonic. Mix in a few extra whole berries and garnish with leaves of thyme.

Sip and contemplate the magnificence of your herb spiral.

Rainwater Harvesting

SWALES & RAIN GARDENS

When it comes to growing anything, it's all about water. You want to catch every drop of it. Moisture in the soil builds organic matter and fertility, which equals naturally healthy plants. Regardless of what you intend to grow, shaping your landscape to harvest the water is step numero uno.

Contrary to modern landscape design that does its best to get rid of water as quickly as possible, we want to look at our homescape as a mini watershed where not one drop of water is going to leave. This goes for all of that overflow coming in from the neighbors, too; that problem is about to become a solution.

So what does this have to do with creating a planting bed? Everything. You want your beds to water themselves and pump fertility naturally. Most raised beds you see are boxed up, and while that is a step in the right direction, you are still being 'square' and missing the flow.

Capture It! How it Works

1. Find Level Ground
2. Dig out a Basin
3. Mound the Sod & Soil Downslope
4. Shape the Bed
5. Fill the Basin with Chips
6. Let the Rain Fall!

Excavating basin and forming berm.

Swale passively harvesting rainwater runoff.

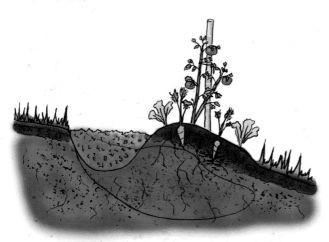

Captured water recharging ground water.

Raised beds on contour not only look beautiful and curvy on your landscape, they also hold and sink the rain. A bed on contour is perfectly perpendicular to the slope, and each point along it is the same level. Unlike conventional swales, which are set off contour to push water away, swales on contour do the opposite by slowing and infiltrating the water right where it is needed most: your garden. To avoid confusion and help you visualize how to create these curvy beauties, I will use the terms "basin" and "berm."

Water zooming down and off your landscape falls into the dug-out portion of the swale—a.k.a., the basin—which is cut on level contour so the water stops and sinks in. This slow infiltration recharges the water table for a broad area stretching downslope of the swale. Like an underground plume, the absorbed rainwater hydrates and recharges the water table under your beds and beyond, making your or your neighbor's yard verdant. Add a good layer of mulch to the raised bed—the berm—to hold in the harvested water and dramatically reduce, if not eliminate, the need to water, even in the driest of summers. With the texture of the basin and berm, you are also creating micro-climates that favor humidity and temperature control, what plants love.

A drop in the bucket

If you have a rain barrel, then you have seen how it fills and overflows within minutes of a good downpour . . . it's just a drop in the bucket! Beyond the barrels and cisterns imagine how much water is falling on and flowing off your yard. This often forgotten zone of rainwater harvesting is a huge source of passive irrigation that can "catch" and sink water into the landscape much like a sponge, harvesting up to 10 times more runoff than a rain barrel. By shaping your landscape to catch and sink the rain, it becomes not only a lush oasis, but also part of the community flood control system. You can even overflow your barrel into a swale or rain garden. This will earn you high water-harvesting Ninja points!

Materials for Swale Building

- ❑ Three pieces of thin scrap wood
- ❑ String level (small mason level 2-3")
- ❑ Landscape flags
- ❑ Shovel
- ❑ Metal rake
- ❑ Compost
- ❑ Newspaper
- ❑ Straw
- ❑ Miscellaneous rocks, any shape, 6"-8"+
- ❑ Woodchips/Mulch
- ❑ Optional: pick ax

Kitchen garden on contour capturing roof and hardscape runoff.

Getting Started

SITING

Swales go just about anywhere they are needed, as long as the slope does not exceed a 3:1 ratio, meaning not more than 1 foot of drop over a 3 foot run. Any steeper than this and you risk blowout from too much water buildup, overflow, and soil destabilization. Terraces are recommended for steep slopes and act in a similar way as the swales in harvesting water on level ground.

Where you begin and end your raised bed on contour is up to you; there are no magic set points where you are supposed to start or finish. Raised beds on contour are often sited based on the restrictions of the surrounding landscape; i.e., walkway, property edge, drive, or fencing. They can be four feet long or extend all the way across your acreage. If possible site your swales for gardens right outside the kitchen window. Outside the window often means close to the roof, patio, and driveway, where rainwater is abundant and meals can be inspired by seeing what is ready to harvest. Just be sure that the swale is located at least 10 feet away from the house.

For larger yards it is good to try and install a swale at the highest point of your land in order to slow the flow as soon as possible and manage water coming in from offsite. Though this may not be the ideal site for your garden, it can be planted with fruit trees, bushes, flowers, or thorny berries as a natural barrier.

If you have sitting water near your foundation, consider putting in a French drain to pull the water away to a point where you can sink it into a swale or rain garden. Sloping your swale slightly off contour to move the bulk of the water to a capture area is also an option.

GETTING LEVEL – A FRAME

In map jargon, contour is the squiggly line that holds the same elevation across a slope. It is rarely a straight line but seems to flow up and down as it finds the level on uneven surfaces and subtle ridges. Finding contour is easy. You don't need fancy gadgets or train-

ing, just a good old-fashioned A frame. This prehistoric tool will get you level. The A frame can be any height you'd like. I usually make mine about four feet tall.

Begin by selecting three thin pieces of wood, ideally scrap, or straight pieces of bamboo, all the same length. Next take two pieces of the wood or bamboo and lay them flat on the ground. Screw the two pieces together at one end. Spread the legs approximately three feet and make a mark one-third the distance up from the bottom on one leg. At this mark, screw on one side of the third length, which becomes the cross piece.

Now, take thin strips of electrical tape and strap a string level to the center of the cross piece. Find a completely level surface, such as the garage floor and stand your (almost) A frame up. Slide the free end of the cross piece slowly up and down the opposite leg, looking for the bubble to sit level. When it does, mark the free leg where the cross piece sits. Pinch it and screw it to the second leg. Bingo! You have a leveling tool. Feel free to cut off any excess length of the cross piece that sticks out past the legs.

WHERE TO BEGIN

At the spot where you want the bed to begin, insert a small landscape flag and place one foot of the A frame next to it. Swivel the other leg in the direction you want to site the swale and slowly move it across the ground until the bubble on the cross piece reads level; mark that leg with another flag. Swivel again and repeat, placing a flag at every leg. Simple and beautiful. Now, don't be surprised if the level takes you in radically different directions than you expected. Depending on your landscape, the line of flags will flow anywhere from almost straight (flat land) to undulating curves (sloped and varied land). Often you end up with a really beautiful serpentine shape flowing across the yard. If the contour leads you into an area that doesn't jibe, adjust your starting point and keep laying the flags until it fits and you like the placement. This is when you can play with where you set the beds and how they look on your landscape. If your A frame lands on a rock or hole, just scoot the whole frame a bit to get past it; otherwise, you won't get an accurate reading.

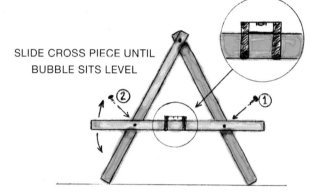

SLIDE CROSS PIECE UNTIL
BUBBLE SITS LEVEL

Diggin' In—Shaping the Swale

Swales come in every size, from huge petrol-machine-carved ones to back yard beauties created with a shovel and a little bean power. It's the latter we will cover here. So eat your beans, grab a shovel, and let's get to it.

Digging the Basin

Approximately 20 inches upslope of the flags, you'll start digging. Dig out the sod up to the flags and flip the grass chunks upside down on the downslope side of the flags, no further than 3 feet away for garden beds. The flipped chunks of sod become the first layer in the forming berm. As you keep digging out the basin, throw the earth on top of the inverted sod.

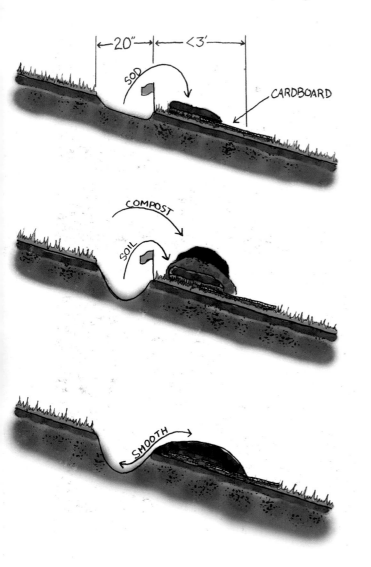

I keep my garden berms at a maximum of 3 feet wide so that I can easily reach in without trampling the soil and plants; remember this as you lay the flipped sod. The bottom of the basin does not need to be perfectly even, but testing it with the A frame or long level is helpful to make sure you are close. The width and height of the berm is in direct relation to the basin size. A wider and deeper basin equals a wider and taller berm; a 6-inch-deep-by-20-inch-wide basin gives you roughly a 3-foot-wide-by-9-inch-high bed, once amended.

Note: If your soil is exceptionally hard, the flat-headed part of a pick ax works great.

The dug-out basin is now your passive water harvester and pathway. I like to fill mine with large wood chips; mulch, pine needles, and leaves also work well. This is mostly to create a nice walking surface and look, but the added organic matter also holds moisture, which maintains a humid micro-climate that the plants love. Depending on how weedy the site is, I often place cardboard in the bottom of the basin before putting in the chips. Over time, the path composts down, adding more fertility and water retention to the surrounding gardens. And to really stack your functions here, if the berm is planted with shade-casting bushes or trees, the chips can be inoculated with the tasty wine cap mushroom. Ninja mulching at its best!

Note: Lay down cardboard over the outer edge of where the raised bed will lay, approximately two to four feet from the flags downslope, before beginning to dig the basin. This will be your grass barrier once the bed is completed, ready to be nicely mulched and frame in the new bed. After the basin is dug, edge back 4 inches of the grass along the flag line so that it doesn't re-sprout or stick out of your final bed.

THE RAISED BED

The pile of sod and soil you have roughly piled up now needs some amending and Zen-shaping. I dump on our local municipal leaf grow compost, which is basically composted leaves and grass, by the wheelbarrow full so that I have a 3:1 ratio of soil to compost (or two-thirds soil to one-third compost). I intimately mix the compost with the loose soil, trying to avoid bringing up the chunks of sod. This is a jump start to feeding your soil and creating a nice planting bed. Once mixed in, it's time to shape it up.

Compost ready to mix in the mounded soil from the dug-out basin.

The goal here is to shape the bed in a flowing pattern, much like a rolling hill with no high drop-off edges. As a general guide, make the width of the berm four times its height; for example, if the berm height is nine inches high, then make the berm width three feet wide. Using a short-tined metal rake, your goal is to make the top of the berm smooth so that falling rainwater settles evenly. This is Zen raking, where being meticulous is actually meditative. Don't fret some soil cascading down; over a season, the soil will "glue" together as it aggregates, and the overall height will come down some with time.

Always plan for an overflow. If your swale is hit with a crazy storm surge or will be receiving a high volume of water, plan how to direct and catch the

Raised bed berms evenly raked into smooth flowing planting surfaces.

overflow. I place overflows where I will want a pathway across the top of the bed, approximately every 20 feet along the berm. Choose your best path-crossing spot on the berm and remove one-third the height of the mixed soil/compost; make the path about 20 to 24 inches wide. Place rocks of any shape along the bottom and sides of the newly excavated path/overflow. Alternatively you can also wait and see where your new berm will naturally want to overflow after a big rain and then build in the path.

I often design multiple swales, one right after the other, to assure capturing every drop of runoff water, and they look beautiful waving across the yard together. When I do this, I just copy the shape of the first swale on contour as it is catching the bulk of water and ideally offset the overflows on each consecutive berm. On a larger landscape, you'll want to space out your swales to take advantage of the rainwater capture area between them. This distance varies depending on the slope of the land. The steeper the landscape, the closer the swales; a general way to site the distance is to walk down-slope until your eye level is equal to the site of the swale above. Place your next swale here.

Planned overflows can also double as pathways.

Notes: If your site for a swale is already downhill and receiving a lot of water from the surrounding properties, beef up the swale size, plan multiple overflows, and place rocks in the basin where the brunt force of the water is entering the swale. The bottom picture here shows where the neighbor's yard practically funnels water into their first swale. Rocks sitting in the basin break up the speed and flow of water.

Your berm and basins do not have to be created all at one time. You can start with a small goal of just a few feet, then when you need the therapy, your eyes are crossing from staring at the computer, and your bum's numb from sitting too long, go back outside and whack away at it—it does wonders!

Additional stones in the basin and beefed up swale size help buffer large volumes of water.

Mulches

Let your mulch serve as your fertilizer. Your soil health is a balance of moisture and organic matter that support the soil life pumping out the fertility. You just about always want your soil to be protected and covered. This simple act makes all the difference in successful growing. For the swale berm that has just been constructed and nicely mixed in with compost, I first lay on newspaper (a.k.a., worm food). The newspaper has multiple functions, but primarily it blocks out the weed seed and grass while trapping the moisture stored in the swale.

Lay the newspaper on, generously overlapping full sections. Lay them so they cascade down the edge of the bed into the basin, giving you coverage from side sprouts and cultivating more growing space. Before going too far down the bed, lay on straw to completely cover and hold down the print. Newspaper that has been left out in the rain to soak lays much easier, especially on a windy day. This simple newspaper and straw mulch will help keep your beds balanced in fertility. At the season's end, I simply throw on an inch or two of compost, newspaper, and straw onto the bed to set the stage for next year's growing. If your site is windy, place branches down on the straw or crisscross the beds with bamboo poles, staked down with short pieces of bamboo.

Planting

To plant plugs or potted plants into the mulch, poke a hole through the soft decomposing paper, plug in the plant, water deep, and tuck back the newspaper and straw. For seeds, do the same; poke a hole and seed, but keep the paper to the side, lightly replace the straw, and beef up the straw again once sprouted. The harvested rainwater in the swale, combined with a good mulch, will help assure an even moisture level even in the driest periods.

Notes: If your mulch is deep, keep a little bucket of compost/soil mix handy when seeding and place a handful in the hole; otherwise, the seed may be too far down from the

The Starter Swale

The super easy start is to build a short five- or six-foot mini swale to catch your downspout water. Measure out about 15 feet (must be a minimum of 10 feet) from the house and downspout and mark out a smiley face, like arms spread to catch the water from the downspout. After you see how well it works, you can add another below it a little longer to catch the overflow; before you know it, you will have a self-watering garden!

Full sections of moist newspaper cascading down side of swale.

Beds well covered with newspaper and straw protect soil and almost always eliminate weeds. Note center bed planted with perennials.

Perennial bed within annual garden for insect habitat and balance.

light. Once the beds are established and you don't have high competition from weeds, you can opt out of the newspaper for direct seeding. The only time I will remove mulch is on beds already a few years old in the early spring, when I want to warm the soil and get germination going.

Perennial Habitat

For annual gardens, I always dedicate a perennial bed or border. Balancing your garden's health means having habitat for beneficial insects, pollinators, lizards, amphibians, and birds all year round. Too often you see the neat and tidied up annual garden put to sleep over the winter without a twig, stone, or stalk to offer protection for our beneficial allies, leaving you to do all their work. So, unless you are masochistic about extra work, plant up some habitat. My garden has a perennial bed in the middle planted with asparagus, strawberries, yarrow, echinacea, comfrey, lovage, hibiscus, lavender, and good king henry that I just let go wild. I don't trim down the dead stalks at season's end or tidy it up at all. The results are a balanced insect ecology in the garden. I also place little piles of rocks on my beds as mulch and habitat. Moisture condenses under the rocks, balances the surrounding temperature, and creates a great lizard habitat. Rocks in the garden make a big difference, even if just piled up in the corner. My gardens also have good bird perches, usually the locust fence posts; native bee habitat (drilled firewood); brush piles; and herb spirals. These all help guarantee beneficial habitat and garden health without my ongoing input, aka work. I don't water, weed, spread fertilizer, or spray my gardens. I just sow, harvest, and enjoy.

Strawberry Rhubarb Whiskey Sour

This recipe has come about from a natural evolution of planting my swales up with strawberries, rhubarb, and a love for whiskey. The strawberries make a great edible ground cover, the rhubarb is deer resistant, and the whiskey . . . it just goes well after a day of toil in the soil.

The essence of this fantastic drink is the rhubarb simple syrup muddled up with a few strawberries, lemon, and mint. The result is a sizzling red delight perfectly balanced between sweet and sour.

INGREDIENTS – MAKES 2 DRINKS

- ❑ 2 oz. rhubarb syrup
- ❑ 6 lemon wedges
- ❑ 8 mint leaves
- ❑ 3 strawberries
- ❑ 3 oz. bourbon
- ❑ Sprigs of mint for garnish
- ❑ 2 strawberries for garnish

RHUBARB SYRUP – MAKES 4 CUPS

- ❑ 4 rhubarb stalks
- ❑ ½ vanilla bean
- ❑ 4 cups water
- ❑ 4 cups sugar

PUT IT TOGETHER

Cut the rhubarb into ½ inch pieces and simmer in water with the vanilla bean and sugar for 20 minutes, stir occasionally. Cool and strain. In the bottom of a mixing glass or jar, muddle (press) the strawberries, lemon, mint and rhubarb syrup. Add in the bourbon and ice, shake, and strain into glass of your choice. Garnish with mint sprig and strawberry. Ahh . . . gardener's delight!

Home-scale rain gardens do not need to be complexly engineered designs or relegated to just plain old non-edible natives. They can be colorful, edible oases that combine form and function.

Rain Gardens

Rain gardens basically are upside-down baseball mitts in the ground, water-sinking depressions that come in many shapes and forms. They are simple imitations of how a forest floor absorbs and sinks rainwater through porous soil. Since society has chopped down our forests and erected suburbia in its place, it's now our role to sink the rain. Lets explore how it's done with function and style.

During a good rain, our homescapes are hit with thousands of gallons of water that rush downstream lickity split. Maybe you have a rain barrel or two that catch a few drops, but most of it is going down the gutter across the landscape and into the watershed, picking up all the funky funk on the way. Hopefully, you are catching some of it with swales on contour, but by adding rain gardens to your landscape you increase your site's multifunctional design while stewarding our watersheds.

Usually rain gardens are sized for the amount of runoff from a site, but you can start small, sink what you can, and build in an overflow. Perhaps you'll

Lack of water-harvesting design loses valuable water and contributes to unfiltered runoff.

decide to create a series of small rain gardens over time and assure every drop of water is staying on your site. The only rule I will give is to start at least 10 feet from your house foundation, unless you are wanting to grow mushrooms in your basement!

Digging it Out

Smaller rain gardens can be dug by hand, such as the one in the top image here, which is approximately 8-by-6-feet-by-24 inches deep. If you go any bigger than that, you'd best be eating your beans or renting a mini-excavator. Yes, you can rent machinery with nothing other than a credit card, and they are fun. The mini-excavator can fit through a 50-inch-wide opening and sneak into tight spaces. They cost around $150 a day, and one day is plenty of time to dig out a small rain garden or two. The three-tiered rain garden and French drain shown on page 36 was dug out with a mini excavator in just one day. Regardless of width, deeper is usually better with 2 feet deep an average for home scale rain gardens. Leave 6 to 12 inches from ground level down to the soil mix; this is called the pooling area, and it allows water to accumulate and sink. If you build the rain garden and fill it to the surface with the rain garden soil mix, it will only harvest what falls on it and runs across it.

Note: Remember to call your utility company before digging. Most will come out for free and mark where you have electric, gas, and water lines running on your property.

There are equations for factoring rainwater runoff—volume relative to rain garden size—but more often than not, residential rain gardens are factored by the available area, budget, and interest

Small teardrop rain garden excavation by hand harvests a considerable amount of runoff.

This small rain garden at the head of an edible woodland garden I designed for Volt restaurant sinks the runoff from the parking lot and overflows into the swales behind.

of the owner. This is totally fine. A rain garden does not need to capture the full amount of water running off your property; any water capture is a benefit. Just plan where the overflow will go.

Soil Mix Recipe

There are two approaches to creating your rain garden soil mix: (1) either mix sand and compost into your existing soil or (2) remove the existing soil altogether and replace it with a pre-made soil, sand, and compost mix from a local landscape supplier. Both are called "engineered" soil, but that's just fancy jargon. They are simply fast-draining soil mixes that imitate the forest floor. Depending on the site, there are pros and cons to both. I prefer to excavate the soil, using the removed sod and soil on my hugelkultur beds* or berming it around the rain garden to add to the rainwater capture. Then I order a soil that I know has been well and evenly mixed. (* see chapter on Hugelkultur.)

Whether you mix it yourself or order it to be mixed and delivered, your goal is to have a well-draining soil. There are many engineered mixes out there; most are designed to very quickly drain out huge amounts of water and be planted with super drought-tolerant

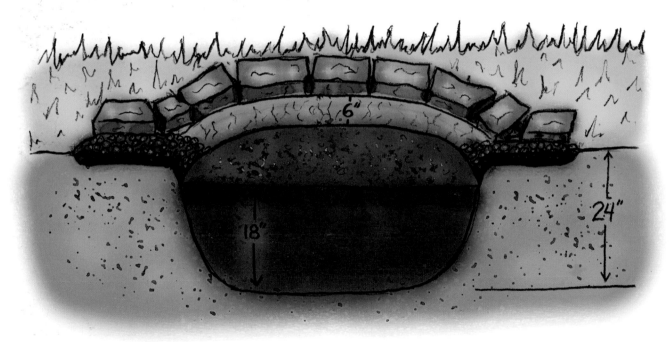

This illustration shows the minimum recommended depths for a rain garden. The 18-inch depth is where the soil mix sits and the top 6-inch drop for water to temporarily pool and sink. Small stone placed at inflow and outflow to avoid erosion. Larger stones can make a nice bed edge and safety from the slight dropoff. Total depth is 24 inches.

plants because the mix is mostly sand. This can be played with and tailored to the plants you want to grow. I like my rain gardens to pump fruit and other lush plants while sinking the runoff, so I balance my soil mixes to both drain and hold some moisture. My favorite combo to date is 50% sand, 25% compost, and 25% top soil.

Even if your local landscape material supplier has never heard of a rain garden or soil mix for one, they are usually happy to custom mix whatever you want. Just ask for the above ratio well-mixed by the cubic yard. A smaller rain garden, such as the one shown on page 33 used approximately 2 yards of mixed soil. Remember to leave the soil surface a good 6 inches below the surrounding ground level and place rock or stones where the water is flowing in and out.

The client on the left, ninja bog gardener Sandi Gill-Smith, had a home built next to her that thoughtfully drained all their water to her side yard. She also had considerable runoff coming from her roof drains and back yard and was dealing with water sitting alongside the house. See how we harvested all the water on the next page.

To capture the large volume of runoff, we designed a three-tiered rain garden that perfectly fit the slope, allowing the water to overflow from one garden to the next, assuring not one drop left the site. Note the French drain coming in from the back yard and moving the stagnant water along the house and leading it into the first bay. The image above right shows the pre-mixed rain garden mix. The image to the right is the completed look with pea gravel surrounding for low maintenance and cut wall stone laid around the edges to help mask the bed edges where the soil drops a good 6 inches once settled. The picture at the beginning of the rain garden section on page 32 is the same design in only its second year of planting!

Planting

The irony of a rain garden is that it is more often than not very dry, thanks to its fast draining character. Unfortunately most rain gardens are only planted up with a handful of drought-tolerant natives when there are loads of function and harvest to be had from all the water capture and loose soil. Some of my rain garden favorites, such as Beach Plum, Juneberry, Elderberry, Aronia, and low bush Blueberry, thrive in the loose and occasionally wet/dry soil. Other beautiful and functional plants to try are Swamp Milk Weed (more attractive than it sounds), Echinacea, Hibiscus moscheutos (edible petals), Winterberry, Spicebush, and Bee Balm to name just a few. For a low-care rain garden, native clump grasses will fill the niche. To balance the periods between rains in the first year, I mulch well and set up a simple drip irrigation or sprinkler as backup.

RESOURCES

Brad Lancaster's "Rainwater Harvesting for Dry Lands and Beyond" volumes 1 & 2 are fantastically written and illustrated. Volume 2 is the real nitty gritty on swale and rain garden design and building.

"The Permaculture Manual" by Bill Mollison & David Holmgren is the bible on overall permaculture design but also detailed in earthworks, swales, rain gardens, etc.

Most states have rain garden publications and non-profits dedicated to helping you get started; many even offer financial support toward your project. See what is going on locally, hopefully you'll be surprised.

'Greening the Desert' YouTube video by Geoff Lawton is an excellent short video on the regenerative benefits of swaling.

Permaculture Ninja

Geoff Lawton is an international leader, designer, and educator in the permaculture movement. His focus on earthworks and water harvesting has transformed even the desert. He is one of the founders of PRI, Permaculture Research Institute, which provides a wealth of permaculture articles at www.permaculturenews.org, and also sells his informative set of permaculture DVD's – one of which is "Harvesting Water - the Permaculture Way." He also has free videos on his site www.geofflawton.com and on YouTube, the most well-known "Greening the Desert" which is only 5 minutes long and pulls many permaculture practices together easily and clearly.

FUNGI!!
GROWING SPECIALTY MUSHROOMS

Outdoor Mushroom Growing

The world of fungi is a fantastic journey of infinite exploration. While that is true, we must limit this chapter to exploring the back yard, homegrown fungi. We will explore the wonders of growing your own tasty mushrooms and how to use them to enhance the overall vitality of your edible landscape. Also, and possibly most importantly, we will explore how we can pair with fungi to help clean up our watersheds.

You may already know the true pleasure of tasting the variety of mushrooms available commercially. This pleasure is nothing when compared to the supreme flavor of wood-grown fungi harvested directly from your back yard.

Back Yard Fungi

I often hear, "My yard is so shady that I can't grow anything." To which I get my big cheesy grin going and say, "Oh yeah you can! Mushrooms love shade!"

Growing mushrooms outdoors is much easier than you may think.

Primarily, I grow three types of mushrooms: shiitake, oyster, and wine cap. These types are easy to grow, tasty, and versatile. I grow shiitake and oyster mushrooms on logs, and the wine cap mushroom, also known as King Stropharia or Garden Giant, I grow on wood chips. All three of these have a wide temperature range for growing as long as there is moisture—make that moisture, moisture, moisture! I If you retain nothing else from this chapter, simply remember: moisture – mushrooms.

Log Culture - The Nitty Gritty

Many types of trees can be used for growing edible mushrooms. In general, you should use hardwoods like maple, poplar, willow, birch, and beech, while avoiding species such as black locust, black walnut, and most evergreens. Our land here in Maryland is rich in tulip poplar and hard maple, perfect for oyster and shiitake, respectively. Oak is the king wood for shiitake, with its thick, protective bark and strong, long-lasting wood. A good oak log can produce beautiful shiitakes for up to eight years, whereas a softer wood like poplar may produce for only three to four years.

Now, you might be thinking, "How is cutting down trees to grow mushrooms ecological?" Our forests have lamentably been chopped down multiple times since the New World began, and the resulting regrowth is usually a cluster of crowded saplings.

A practice of sustainable forestry is the thinning of small diameter trees to allow the larger, more mature trees to grow and to let in more sunlight that helps regenerate the forest floor. These saplings are the perfect size for mushroom log cultivation.

Simply grabbing some old firewood off the pile to grow your mushrooms won't work, since the wood already has its own funky fungi going on. Mushroom wood needs to be fresh and from healthy trees. I cut my wood at winter's end before sap rise, which in Maryland is around the end of February/early March. Trees or branches approximately six inches in diameter are best. A larger diameter is fine if you have the brawn; however, smaller diameters are not recommended, as the wood will dry out too easily. Once downed, I mark and cut the logs at about 40 inches in length, which makes a manageable size to move around. I then leave the logs where they are, slightly lifted off the ground, or move them where it is moist, leaving them for about three weeks. This period allows the tree's natural anti-fungal properties to die off and the temperature to warm up for inoculation in late March or early April.

Note: if you have healthy wood that was downed during the winter, it is usable as long as you inoculate in the early Spring.

Ninja Move: Put spore-inoculated bar oil from Fungi Perfecti* in your chainsaw so that as you cut wood, you seed the stumps and surrounding debris. Throw some sawdust back on the stump to help keep in the moisture.

Maple logs ready to inoculate.

Fungi-Growing Medium

Fungi, the mushroom body, is made up of thread-like cells that weave together to make a network. When ready to fruit and release spores (seed), up pops the edible shoots we love so much. If you have ever kicked aside the leaf litter in a forest and seen the white webbing, then you've seen fungi. We call these threads "mycelium."

For mushroom cultivation, we want specific fungi mycelium (i.e., shiitake and oyster strains). The mycelium growth is started on sawdust, straw, grain, or little wooden plugs. When inoculated with mycelium these mediums are called "spawn." Think of them as kindling to get the mycelium going. For beginning ease, I suggest purchasing spawn with mycelium on them from one of the many fine mushroom supply outfits; ideally, one close to your weather range. I am a big fan of Field & Forest.** Their claim is: "Proud to be part of this rotting world." Their website and online catalog are a perfect package of how-to's and materials for beginners.

There are numerous spawn options, but for small-scale use, I prefer the plug spawn. Plug spawn are little birch dowels that arrive covered in the mycelium variety you choose. These spawn will be inserted into the logs.

*FungiPerfecti.com for chainsaw spores and a universe of mushroom supply and info

**Field & Forest www.fieldforest.net

Plug spawn with mycelium.

Notes

- A log roughly 6 inches in diameter by 40 inches long will take between 30-40 plug spawn. 250 plugs run about $20.

- There are shiitake and oyster varieties that fruit at different temperature ranges, offering extended harvest throughout the growing season (early spring to late fall).

- Spawn can be ordered a month or so in advance and kept refrigerated.

- You can also collect your own spores from local fruiting varieties (which has the benefit of being a more resilient strain).

- I highly recommend reading "Mycelium Running: How Mushrooms Can Help Save the World," by Paul Stamets. I consider this to be the bible on mushroom cultivation and use.

Setting Up the "Shroom Zone"

Before the big bucks start to roll in from your mushroom sales, a bare bones work area is needed. Come late March/early April, I set up my super low-tech mushroom inoculation area outside the garage. It's comprised of a few straw bales laying flat, a strong electric drill, a hammer, an old camping stove, and a nasty old fondue pot.

Material List

- ☐ Hardwood logs (6 inches by 40 inches)
- ☐ $\frac{5}{16}$" wood drill bit
- ☐ Electric drill
- ☐ Straw bales as work bench or other low surface to work on
- ☐ Hammer
- ☐ Camping stove or other outdoor heating source
- ☐ Wax (cheese or bees)
- ☐ A small bristle brush, small paint brush, or wax dauber
- ☐ Spawn
- ☐ Good beer
- ☐ Optional: metal label tags

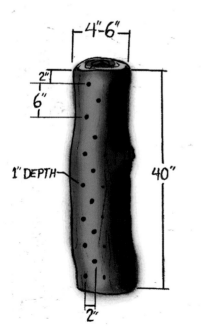

Drilling Pattern

Drilling Diamonds

Once you have your shroom zone set up and first brew poured, it's time to arm yourself with a drill. The logs are going to be drilled in a diamond pattern for the plug spawn. Start the first row two inches from the log's end. Space the holes every six inches. The depth of the hole is important. Ideally, the plug will be inserted to a depth just below the bark, almost flush, but not sticking out, about 1 inch deep. Field & Forest sells ninja drill bits that have stoppers on them for the correct depth, but I have used a piece of tape or a pen mark on the bit to eyeball the depth. It's good to drill a few holes and check the depths by tapping in the spawn to see how it fits. Soon, you'll get the feel for it. Use caution not to drill too deep, as that leaves a dry air pocket.

Once you have your first row done, rotate the log two inches and begin the next row, starting between the first two holes of the previous row, approximately five inches down. Continue rotating the log two inches for every new row and offsetting the holes to create a diamond pattern. The inches here are approximate, so don't get worked up, just pull on the brew for balance. Drilling this many holes is a bit overkill, but it's necessary to make sure that our chosen fungi is the one that colonizes and out-competes any other funky airborne fungi.

Drilling log with good beer.

Whacking in spawn plugs is fun. Those skills you built up playing the fair game Whack a Mole are about to pay off. As fun as whacking stuff may be, we need to be careful not to damage the bark. The bark on your log is the skin that keeps the moisture in, so handle it gently. Oaks, with their thick bark, are favored in this process; poplars, with thin and brittle bark, not so much. Some folks recommend using rubber mallets, but I find workshop participants tossing them aside in favor of the metal hammer. Now, armed with your hammer and bag of spawn, let's get to it. Keep in mind that the bag of spawn is sensitive to drying out and should be protected from sun and wind while working.

About the time I'm ready to start whacking in spawn, I set up my hybrid wax-melting station. This station uses an old Coleman, two-burner propane gas stove. I set this up about 20 feet from the drilling and whacking stations, as the wax smoke can get thick and the wax will inevitably drip. I've seen set-ups in the garage with a plug-in burner and tarp underfoot, but that somehow loses the outdoors mystique. Both approaches work. For a pot, I use an old fondue pot, but really any pot will do. Some more legit folks might recommend using a double boiler and putting water in the bottom of the first pot or even just placing a metal bowl in a pot with water as a makeshift double boiler.

Whacking in spawn plug.

I use a cheese wax that I get in big chunks cheaply from Field & Forest, and it seems to last forever. Start off with a fist-sized chunk. I crank the heat to medium high and watch until the wax melts clear and starts to fine bubble. Then, turn the heat to low, around 300 degrees. You want the wax to be as hot as possible without catching on fire. I judge the heat by the smoke; a thin smoke is good, while a thick one is getting close to the flash point. Often during workshops, where I have a small army of first-time drillers and whackers, I forget to turn the wax down and it catches on fire. It's no huge blaze, but you cannot salvage the wax once it's caught fire. I carefully take it off the burner, dump it on the gravel drive, and start again. The flash point is easier to control

Waxing logs.

with a double boiler set up. The trick is to have the wax as hot as possible to ensure a good seal that traps moisture and keep critters out; otherwise, the wax can dry and peel off. Once your wax is hot, use a small bristle brush, a steel baster, or wax daubers (which are a dollar a pop from Field & Forest) to dab the wax over each spawn.

If you have, or plan to have, multiple types of mushrooms, it is a good idea to label the logs with aluminum tags nailed into the log's end. Put the type, variety, and date. It will help to track what does well, to make recommendations to others and be sure you are harvesting the right fungi.

A Shady Place for Some Shady Characters

The next stage in the fungi journey is one of the most critical: the spawn run. This is when the mycelium jumps off the spawn into the log and begins to colonize it. This can take anywhere from six to eighteen months. Be patient and have faith. Place the logs flat during the spawn run, just off the ground an inch or two. Moisture during this time is key. The logs want to be placed in a shady place that imitates a forest setting, out of the wind, and, ideally, close to the house and watering source. If you have a naturally moist, shady area around your house, that is a good spot. My new favorite place to stash logs is under the deck, where water falls through and the house blocks the wind. The fungi love it! Another good spot is underneath evergreens that are porous and allow enough water to fall through. You can create your own shade with a 60-80 percent shade cloth draped over straw bales with logs laid in between.

Keep your logs moist, water like your garden. If there has been no rain, they need the equivalent of about one inch of water a week. You can either hose them and the area around them down once a week, or set up a sprinkler and run it for 15-20 minutes. Once the logs fruit, lean them up to view and easily harvest the mushrooms.

Logs under deck during spawn run.

Leaning logs ready to fruit under evergreens.

Working with fungi is one of the rare win, win, win scenarios where every step of the process has a myriad of benefits. By thinning trees for growing mushrooms, you help rebalance the forest; by inoculating wood with fungi, you speed up the soil building process; and by spreading more fungi in the landscape, you strengthen ecosystems and increase runoff filtration. On the economic side, growing mushrooms for market is as lucrative as a legal crop gets. Local farmers markets and restaurants pay top dollar for outdoor fungi. Value add the harvest into a bottled sauce or oil and you'll be rolling.

Harvest & Use

When the logs fruit, usually after a warm spring or fall rain, simply cut the mushrooms off at the base, being careful to not pull off chunks of the bark. Then, the sky's the limit for enjoying and preserving them. You will be amazed at the abundance a log produces at once. If you can get past sautéing them in butter and garlic or making creamy mushroom soup, then they are easy to dry and store. My personal favorite preservation is shiitake vodka! But for you teetotalers, a mushroom-infused olive oil with peppercorns and hot peppers is a tasty treat and great gift.

A Word About Mushroom Safety

You may be wondering if is safe to eat any ol' mushroom that grows out of the log. The answer is an emphatic "Hell No!!"

If your spawn variety has not successfully run and colonized the log, it's possible that another airborne fungi has set up shop. Only harvest the type that you inoculated the log with and have a picture of what that is. If you inoculate a shiitake, only harvest a shiitake. Oysters and shiitake are easy to identify. The beauty of growing your own mushrooms versus hunting for them is that you know exactly what is supposed to pop out.

Getting Stumped, Growing Mushrooms on Stumps

Many times, these treasure chests of mushroom wood are overlooked when inoculating. To forget inoculating the tree stumps is passing up the easiest and most abundant harvests that last for years. The stumps have a huge amount of wood mass and roots for the fungi to colonize and pull moisture from.

Start by cutting a two- or three-inch round off the stump. Again be sure the wood is healthy and recently cut, otherwise other ambient fungi will have already moved in.

You've probably seen mushrooms popping out of stumps in copious amounts. I remember one morning in town my ol' hound dog Chulo led me to this huge clump of oyster mushrooms growing out of the stump he was sniffin' about. The old stump was a fungi treasure hidden in the grass. I lopped the shrooms off and traded them for breakfast at the café down the street.

Cherry stump drilled along edge and filled with Reishi mushroom spawn plugs.

Then, similar to the log inoculation method using plugs, drill every two inches around the face edge of the cut stump. Hammer in the plugs, and then nail the round back onto the stump to sandwich in the spawn. Alternatively, you can put in sawdust spawn like the totem method described below. The spawn inoculation in a stump can take a lot longer to run than the logs, but once set, fruiting can last into the next decade.

Totem Method

A few years back, I was talking on the phone with Joe Krawczyk, founder of Field & Forest and co-author of "Year-Round Shiitake Cultivation in the North." I was telling him about my abundant poplar forest and my goal to inoculate it with oyster mushrooms. He shared a fantastic method that fruitfully marries the two together: Mushroom Totems! The ultimate shrine to the mushroom god. Alas, the totem method still relies on chainsaws but requires a lot less work overall and yields big returns.

Poplar totem with oyster spawn.

Materials

- ❑ Sawdust spawn
- ❑ 12" log rounds
- ❑ Black plastic lawn-size garbage bags
- ❑ Paper grocery bag
- ❑ String

Cut the logs from healthy, dormant trees at winter's end. You will need two log pieces that are approximately 12 inches in diameter by 12 inches long. In the bottom of a black plastic lawn-size bag, spread out a handful of sawdust spawn, about a cup's worth. Set the first log round on top of the sawdust. Spread another handful or two on top of the log, approximately a quarter-inch thick, and place the second log on top of it. Repeat with another ¼-inch layer, then cover the top with a brown paper grocery bag secured with string or a large rubber band. Alternatively you can cut a 2-inch round and nail to the top as seen in the picture on the right.

Oyster totem after 3 months, covered in mycelium!

Oysters popping from totem piece planted a few inches in the ground.

Totem pieces happily seated under the deck.

Pull the black plastic bag up around your finger and tie closed, leaving just the small opening where your finger was for breathing. Stash this magical totem where the temps stay within 60 to 80°F for about three months. I put mine in the basement boiler room during the spring or summer (when the boiler is not in use) and in the garage (when the boiler is fired up). Really, anywhere indoors and out of the way is fine. Forget about it for three months, and when you come back to it and unwrap it, you'll find it coated in white mycelium.

Take each log round and place on the ground with your other logs. I put mine down a few inches into the soil under the deck, and they love it, popping crazy amounts of mushrooms. The advantages of totem method include: less work than drilling; no whacking or waxing; guaranteed moisture and temperature during spawn run; and thick, long-lasting chunks of wood. The only disadvantages are finding a place to stash them indoors and using plastic bags.

Notes

- You can place just one log piece in the plastic bag, if moving the two together isn't practical.
- Shiitake and Lion's Mane can also be done as totems.
- A five-pound bag of sawdust spawn, which costs about $25, is enough to inoculate six double-decker totems.

Wine Cap: King Stropharia

True to its name, wine cap mushrooms are a pleasure to consume and a breeze to grow. Also known as Garden Giant or King Stropharia, this mushroom can grow as big as five pounds! They are succulent, taste meaty, slightly nutty, and delicious. Very easy to grow—and no chainsaw is needed! Unlike the log-culture method of growing mushrooms, wine cap inoculation can be started throughout the season and only needs wood chips and dappled light to flourish. And, boy, are they fast to fruit! A planting in early spring can fruit that same season, although occasionally they can take a full 12 months to bear fruit.

I get my wood chips dropped for free from a local arborist. All I ask is that they are not pine or from the side of the highway (sprayed with chemicals). The fresher, the better; but chips up to three months old will still work fine.

Wine cap mushroom.

Fast Growing Mushrooms

Oysters and shiitakes are also easily grown on straw outdoors. It takes additional steps to pasteurize the straw before inoculation, but the return harvests are generous and pop up in as little as three weeks! Paul Stamets' book "Mycelium Running" has great coverage and alternative methods for straw cultivation.

Oyster mushrooms growing in straw-filled bags in the outdoor shower at the Bullock Bros Homestead on Orcas Island – the premier permaculture haven. www.permacultureportal.com. If you make it there, just ask for Cosmic Bob.

Materials:

- Cardboard
- Wood chips
- Spawn
- Straw

The Mushroom Patch

The wine cap mushroom patch can be any shape you'd like. You can make it a new mulch ring for a much-loved tree or as a stamp shape under a setting of deciduous trees. I often fashion mine as I do for food forest patches, about 10 feet by 10 feet. If the site is not completely bare to the soil, I put down cardboard first to reduce competitor fungi then dump the wood chips on top about two inches thick. If the chips are not moist, be sure to wet them thoroughly with a hose as they go down. For the first planting, you will start with a bag of sawdust spawn from a supplier. After that, you should never again need to buy spawn, as the patch easily self-propagates.

A 5.5-pound bag of sawdust spawn, which runs about $25, will cover at least 50 square feet. With that in mind, sprinkle out half the total dose of sawdust onto the moist chips. Next, drop on another two inches of moist chips and add the second half of the spawn to the top. Mix in the spawn on top a little with a metal rake or by hand. Last, sprinkle on fresh straw and water down. Do not worry if the straw begins to sprout; it will only help the wine cap trap more moisture.

Keep the patch moist as you would your garden. Expect flushes of mushrooms throughout the season from late spring to fall; wine cap has a wide range of fruiting temperatures (40°F to 90°F). After the first fruiting, either feed the patch more wood chips or scoop a bucketful from the mycelium-rich patch and start a new one, using a ratio of approximately 1:20 (or one bucket of spawn to 20 buckets of new chips). Or let it go and plant right into the rich compost it has created.

Without continued feeding, the patch will expend itself into fertile compost and stop fruiting. To re-feed the original patch, just dump on 2 to 3 inches of moistened fresh chips, mix in well, and recover with straw.

In mid-summer, once the mycelium has run through the chips, I take a bucketful of mycelium and spread it under my garden veggies, particularly the tomatoes and zucchinis, forming donut shapes around the base of the plants. The leaf coverage and moisture

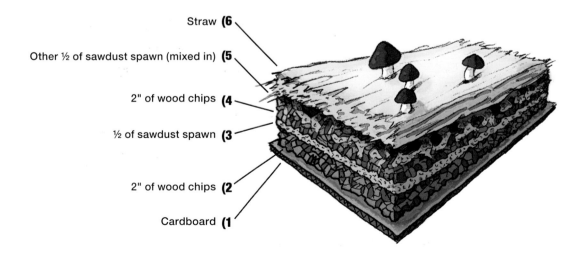

Straw **(6**

Other ½ of sawdust spawn (mixed in) **(5**

2" of wood chips **(4**

½ of sawdust spawn **(3**

2" of wood chips **(2**

Cardboard **(1**

Wine Cap Mushroom Patch.

of the plant is just right for the wine cap to thrive and fruit. It also boosts the plants' nutrient uptake. Then, when I'm out harvesting my dinner, I'm able to easily add in tasty mushrooms!

Siting

Unlike the log culture, your wine cap mushroom patch would like a little interface with light. I place my patches under deciduous trees that interface with the lawn, where moisture seems to naturally cycle. I have also successfully grown wine caps under a shade cloth rigged up out in the middle of a sunny garden. And I have failed when trying to grow them in deep shade, though I did get an awesome compost pile from it. Even a few hours of direct sunlight will not undo the wine cap, but instead help stimulate the moisture flow to the surface where the mycelium is growing.

Wine caps aren't the only shroom that can be grown on woodchip patches. When I cut the driveway through the woods to the circular strawbale house I'm building, I marked it along contour and sited it to pull down the fewest number of trees possible. The trees that did come down got cut into mushroom logs and totem chunks; the rest were chipped into mounds approximately 5 feet by 10 feet by 2 feet high. Into these mounds, which now run all along my drive, I stuck a fruiting oyster totem log round—essentially, a huge spawn plug—and chucked straw over the top. Now all I have to do as I come up the drive is slow down, lean out the truck door, and harvest massive clumps of shelf oysters for the table. Some I let go to release spores and inoculate the surrounding forest debris, eventually saving me from having to do anything but just hike around with my big ol' mushroom-harvesting bag.

Geeky side note of mycelium's benefits in the garden:

Even if you never harvest a mushroom, you'll be creating the most amazing compost on the planet! By incorporating fungi into your landscape and gardens, you boost yields and heal soils. You can forget about fertilizing. Apart from loosening the soil and adding moisture retention, these guys pump carbon dioxide that the plants chug like fuel. It's a dance between plant and fungi, a little sugar flow, or biochemical love exchange.

Notes

- Use mesh bags to harvest mushrooms in so that you are further spreading spores as you walk about.
- Since the wine cap is grown on the ground around other terrestrial fungi, be sure to identify it well before eating.

How to Save the World! Ninja Mushrooms

Paul Stamets* aptly says in his TED talk that, historically, those species that have paired with fungi were rewarded with survival.

We can pair with fungi right at home to help repair our damaged ecosystems and watersheds. Our watershed health begins where we live. The water running off our driveways, roofs, swimming pools, and lawns heads downstream fast. Pairing with fungi, we can filter the funk running onto and off our landscapes—and even the petrochemicals from our cars—very easily.

Multiple classes of fungi can be used to restore our habitats; however, some of the best types are the ones we've just learned about: saprophytic mushrooms, such as oyster and wine cap.

The mycelial matt that is formed on the wood chips acts as a filtering web that traps and consumes a wide range of chemical toxins, silt, and pathogens. A great way to package these mycelium-filters is by stuffing burlap sacks full of wood chips and inoculating with spawn—same idea as the patches. Again, be sure the chips are moist, then insert either a handful of sawdust or plug spawn in the middle as you are filling the bags. Stack the sacks in dappled shade and keep moist for a couple of months, by which time the mycelium has run rampant. Regardless of your spawn success, or even if you don't inoculate the sacks yourself, just placing the chip-filled sacks in the moist shade will cause fungi to come.

These sacks of mycelium filtration can be placed in any number of locations around the landscape. In the pictures on page 53 you can see where I have dug a small trough in the lawn where multiple gutter spouts flush toxic roof runoff into a creek just down slope. I wedged in three sacks filled with wood chips and inoculated with wine cap, covered them with cardboard to add moisture retention, and topped with four inches of woodchips, bringing it all flush with the grass. This simple little myco-remediation patch will make a huge difference in mitigating the toxins in the runoff from the roof. Each year, add a few inches of wood chips to the top layer to maintain the food cycle and moisture for the fungi. This simple design is a huge stewardship for our watersheds whose largest toxic loads come from our homes.

Similarly, placing the sacks along the driveway filters runoff and cleans up our waterways and watersheds. Place the sacks adjacent to the drive where water sheets off and filters through the wood chip media. If the flow is strong at any one point, buffer the in-flow with rocks or line the edge with rocks to help hold in the chips. These filters can be done in a myriad of creative ways that can also become amazing planting beds.

Another efficient way to hold the water on your landscape and filter is to sink this runoff in a raised bed swale. I did a variation of this stacked function in one of my young forest gardens. I marked and carved a swale on contour, creating a raised bed on the downhill side, where I've planted juneberries, paw paws, and persimmons that are beginning to cast shade. In the dugout portion of the swale, which now becomes the path, I put in wood chips and inoculated with wine cap spawn from one of my patches. Using the same idea as the sacks, I cover the inoculated chips with cardboard and then another four inches of chips. There are so many stacked functions to this design: the rainwater runoff held in the swale keeps the chips and fungi moist, the mycelium enriches the soil for the trees, I stimulate the mycelium by walking on it, and the compost it creates I just chuck on the bed and start another fungi path. Love it. That's my kind of ecological footprint.

Notes

- With time, the sacks and chips will break down into organic-rich soil that can be planted and function as a runoff filter with many of the same benefits.
- I get burlap coffee bags from a local organic roaster. Just make sure the sacks aren't treated. If you plan to make multiple sacks, stack un-inoculated filled bags on top of the inoculated ones and the mycelium will jump to them.

*I humbly bow to the Fungi Guru, Paul Stamets, and his unparelled works on the fungi universe. I'm always encouraging folks to give 18 minutes of their life to hear Paul's TED Talk on how mushrooms can save the world. It will blow you away to realize how linked we are with fungi!

Wine cap fungi covering wood chips in burlap sacks just months after inoculation.

Burlap sacks filled with inoculated wood chips filtering roof runoff.

Topped over with chips, easy to mow over.

Food forest swale path inoculated with wine cap mushroom spawn

Maple Mushroom Martini

The magic in this mushroom martini is the infused mushroom vodka. To some this may not sound appealing, but it must be tried. Mushrooms and vodka blend so smoothly and can actually have a tonic effect – magic for the soul and body.

INGREDIENTS - MAKES 1 DRINK

- ❑ 2 oz. mushroom-infused vodka
- ❑ ¾ tsp maple syrup
- ❑ 5-6 dashes orange bitters
- ❑ ½ tbsp fresh squeezed lemon juice
- ❑ 1 dash aromatic bitters

MUSHROOM VODKA

- ❑ ¼ cup dried Chanterelle Mushrooms or fresh* shroom of choice
- ❑ 1 cup vodka

Combine ingredients in a jar, seal, and infuse for about 3 days. Strain.
*If using fresh mushrooms, you will need more, so fill the jar and cover with vodka.

Mix all of the above ingredients in a cocktail shaker or jar with ice.
This drink has the flavor of the mushroom, with a touch of sweetness from the maple, balanced with the tart lemon juice and bitters. In all, I think this was pretty delicious! I wouldn't mind having another.

Cheers!

Both recipe & pic courtesy of Boozed + Infused, Infusing liqueurs at home with inspiring and seasonal ingredients. www.boozedandinfused.com

What do you call a mushroom that walks into a bar and buys everyone a drink? A Fun-gi!

Young food forest planted with a diversity of perennials: Egyptian Walking Onion, gooseberry, wormwood, sage, juneberry . . . .

Food Forests

A Food Forest is a low maintenance gardening technique that mimics a woodland ecosystem but substitutes woodland species with edible trees, bushes, perennial vegetables, herbs, vines, and annuals.

Benefits

There are many benefits to creating food forests:

- Can be squeezed into the smallest of plots
- Can be built around an existing tree
- Create a balanced ecology
- Pump out fruit, nuts, flowers, herbs
- Are simple to create and maintain
- Provide habitat, pollination, fertilizer & pest management

How To Grow a Food Forest?

Food Forests are grown *like* a forest, not in the forest. By observing the natural patterns of a healthy forest ecosystem, we see a lot of intimate, successful relationships. A healthy forest efficiently converts solar energy into biomass, so why not learn from it to grow our own food systems? This may take a moment to process since we are used to hearing and reading about spacing between plants and rows, nutrient and light competition. In short, we have a traditional view of agriculture that holds back natural succession and biodiversity.

When I look at a healthy forest, it looks like everything is blasting out of the same hole! There are tall overstory trees, mid-sized trees, small understory trees, shrubs, herbs, ground covers, and mushrooms, with vines climbing up through it all! It's all pumping and working together, not neatly spaced out. Where there is sufficient water, land wants to become forest and return to ecological diversity. The forest may not necessarily be full of the species we favor for food, medicine, and drinks, but we can take the idea and the pattern and design our own food forest.

Let's take this idea back to square one . . . literally. We're looking at our patch of lawn and thinking, "Yeah, that all sounds groovy, but how do I begin *and* get my neighbors and homeowners association to love it?"

To start, you don't need much space or the tall overstory layer. On smaller acreage it is best to stick with the mid-sized trees – your fruit trees, fruiting bushes, plus the lower-growth plants, herbs, and ground covers to maximize the available light. A food forest can be as small as 8 x 8 feet and be as simple as your favorite small, self-fertile fruit tree surrounded by beneficial perennials. Or you can completely transform your entire yard into a food forest mosaic. But let's start with a simple plan built around good organic fruit tree care with low input.

Design your growing systems to thrive on low input and have more time to swing in the hammock.

What we usually see is one lone fruit tree plopped into a sea of grass in the yard, left to the mercy of marauding weed whackers and lawn mowers. At best, this tree will have a small ring of mulch at its base. So, it's basically left on its own to fight it out with a mono-culture of hungry grass and left to rely on you to feed, water, spray . . . what we refer to as "work"! Now, how does planting the needs of the fruit tree up front and leaving you some more time to swing in the hammock sound?

Material List Per "Patch"

- ❑ Three wheelbarrows of compost/manure
- ❑ A week's worth of newspaper
- ❑ 8-10 mid-sized cardboard boxes
- ❑ Six wheelbarrows of wood chips, mulch, or leaf compost (Deluxe Patch)
- ❑ One bale of straw
- ❑ Fencing (if deer-challenged)

Getting Started

The Food Forest Patch, Starting from Scratch

Start by picking an area that ideally gets at least eight hours of direct sunlight a day. It doesn't matter how challenging the soil is, or what's already growing in or on it. Mark out a square 8 x 8 foot patch—or whatever shape you'd like—with flags, sticks, or you can simply eyeball it. The layer of grass, or whatever is already growing, will become your first layer in the soil building. It is important for you to keep it, as it will add nutrients and organic matter to the upcoming soil building sheet mulch.

Now we begin with the easiest soil building technique on the planet Earth: sheet mulching. Sheet mulching is basically layering various organic materials on the ground to build up soil, hold mois-ture, and block out weeds. Some call it lasagna gar-dening. The recipes to follow are only outlines and can be modified just as you would in the kitchen.

You can sheet-mulch your patch at any time of the year. Ideally the patch is left to decompose for at least one season in advance of planting (i.e., in the fall for spring planting, in spring for fall planting).

Eco-Logical

By observing how natural ecologies function, we can imitate their patterns for the things we need in a human habitat: food, fodder, fiber, medicine, and building materials. A well-designed system supports itself without much human energy and material input. This may sound dynamic and complex, which it is, but getting it started is easy.

Throw down compost, manure . . . yourself.

Generously cover with overlapping newspaper and/or cardboard.

Finished patches ready to sit and decompose.

Leaving it for a full year will yield even better results.

Since I'm like Johnny Appleseed in spreading these patches everywhere, I have municipal leaf compost delivered by the yard. I put down two to three inches over the 8 x 8 foot square, the equivalent of about three wheelbarrows or one-third of a cubic yard. This first layer can be just about any nutrient-rich material, such as fresh cow manure, vegetable waste, your own compost, or leaves. Approximately nine wheelbarrows of compost equals one cubic yard, or enough for three patches.

Next, you will add the layer of newspaper. Take unopened

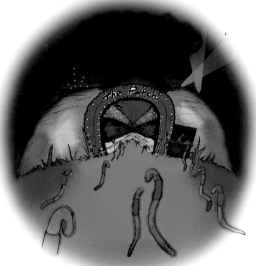

sections of the black and white sections only and place them over the compost, slightly overlapping each section (ideally, each section should be about eight pages thick). If windy, be ready to wet down the paper as you lay it. Even better is paper that has been left out in the rain; it lays and stays much easier. The newspaper provides multiple functions: it helps kill off the grass or weeds beneath and minimizes regrowth, traps moisture, and brings up the worms who love the news. You'll have worms coming from miles around once word gets out about the new editions. As the worms come up from beneath the soil to enjoy the compost and newspaper, they will be tunneling through the hard-packed earth, loosening the soil and fertilizing with their castings. All that for just chucking some compost and recycling materials on the ground!

Note: Newsprint these days is made with soy-based inks, so the worms give it the "organic" stamp of approval. Do not use the glossy inserts, as they are toxic to the soil and the worms. Use the black-and-white sections only.

Next, the recipe can be mixed up, depending on your preferred aesthetics. For example, the front yard versus the back 40. For the suburban-type landscape, the patch can be modified by laying down newspaper in generous amounts (double up the sections) prior to putting down the compost. Finish it off with two to three inches of leaf compost or a compost and top soil planting mix. This design is easier to shape with curves or around existing trees.

Food forests can come in any shape and blend beautifully with existing borders

Starting with lawn, the bed was edged, covered with cardboard and newspaper, then laid over with wood chips as the path, and a soil/compost mix for the planting bed.

Viola! Simply done and crowned with a small herb spiral. The bed is now being planted with woodland edge species, and blending with the tree line along the fence.

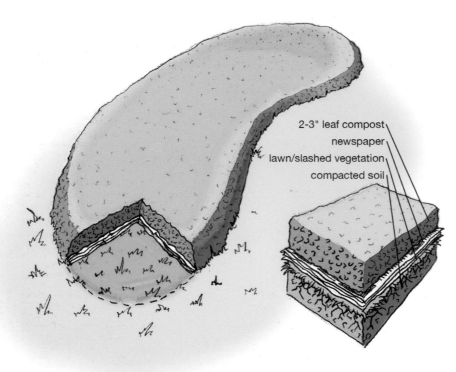

2-3" leaf compost
newspaper
lawn/slashed vegetation
compacted soil

The front yard version.

For the back 40 and where the strength of weed or grass is tough, add a cardboard layer on top of the newspaper that will act as further worm food, a moisture retainer, and weed blocker. Again, be generous with the cardboard and overlap each section. What you top it off with is up to you and can match any aesthetic preference. I like to use straw, as it's easy to apply and breaks down quickly, at the same rate the other layers do. However, mulch, wood chips, pine needles, leaves, top soil or even more leaf compost will do just fine.

Note: Older trees can be retrofitted with sheet mulch out to the drip line for big benefits and added planting space. The lightweight mulch will not inhibit the roots from breathing, rather it will increase porosity. With any sheet mulch design, be prepared to patch up any sprouts of grass or weeds the first season or two with more newspaper and your choice of covering.

Mike's Deluxe Sheet Mulch (a.k.a., Black Gold)

For the Hardcore Ninja Food Forest Enthusiast, I recommend Mike's Deluxe Sheet Mulch, which gives you over two years of soil building at once. Start by following the initial directions above—chuck down your compost layer, newsprint, and cardboard. Follow by adding four inches of wood chips (this is called the "fungal layer"), add another layer of cardboard, and your choice of topping (mulch, more wood chips, leaves, or leaf compost). If you leave out the second layer of cardboard because it is a windy site or you're worried it will become exposed, then double up on the topping.

The added wood chips sandwiched between the cardboard will retain moisture and draw in saprophytic fungi (a.k.a., the wood munchers). As an alternative to wild fungi, which will readily show up to help decompose the wood chips, you can inoculate this layer yourself using the garden giant mushroom (see page 49). The compost and newspaper will feed the worms and soil biota for about a year. By then, the cardboard and wood chips are well into decomposition and continue the soil-feeding cycle and nutrient release to your plants. This makes Black Gold in just a year's time, where only hard, barren soil was before. It really is all about the fungi!

Notes: The wood chips can be of any age, though if you want to inoculate with the garden giant, be sure they are less than six months old and, ideally, hardwood (not pine). I get mine from a local arborist for a 12-pack of beer, as it saves him a trip to the dump. Light beer doesn't work . . . it's a weak trade. For windy sites that blow away the top layers of the sheet mulch while it is still freshly laid, either lay across thick branches or crisscross with bamboo poles that are staked down at the corners. The sheet mulch will eventually hunker down as it gets rained on and begins to decompose.

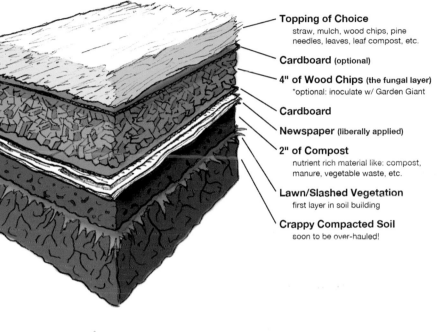

Mike's Deluxe Sheet Mulch

Topping of Choice
straw, mulch, wood chips, pine needles, leaves, leaf compost, etc.

Cardboard (optional)

4" of Wood Chips (the fungal layer)
*optional: inoculate w/ Garden Giant

Cardboard

Newspaper (liberally applied)

2" of Compost
nutrient rich material like: compost, manure, vegetable waste, etc.

Lawn/Slashed Vegetation
first layer in soil building

Crappy Compacted Soil
soon to be over-hauled!

Designing & Planting Your Food Forest

The year after I create the patch, I plant bare root trees in the spring and late fall. Starting in the center of the patch, I stick my shovel into the composted Black Gold like a knife through butter. Then I plant one of my main producers—a fruit or nut tree.

There is a saying that for a five dollar tree you want a twenty dollar hole, meaning dig out a good wide hole for your new tree roots. If you are planting a bare root tree, eyeball or measure the roots' length and width when spread out. Place the bare root tree in a 5 gallon bucket of water while you dig the hole, being sure all the roots are submerged. Only dig your hole as deep as the roots' depth but go extra wide on the width (no limit). Be sure to

Black Gold filled with strands of white mycelium.

keep the sides of your hole vertical; it is natural to dig a bullet-shaped hole that can make the roots slope together rather than spread out into the surrounding soil. It also helps to rough up the sides of the hole with the shovel for the same reason. You will want to spread the roots out so they are completely comfortable and not cramped.

The soil mark should be on the tree where it was dug out at the nursery and that is where you want it to sit again, not lower and not higher. I often place a straight stick or piece of lumber across the hole to see where the soil line will be. Then ideally you have someone helping to hold the tree suspended in the hole at the right height while you slowly fill back in the excavated earth, otherwise hold the tree steady with one hand and fill with the other. Break up any clods, and be sure to fill all gaps around the roots, really getting your fingers in there. If the tree has sunk a bit as you finish filling the hole, you can gently pull and shake to raise it to surface height. If it is set too high, start again.

If your tree is potted, the same applies for the wide hole, roughed up sides, etc. If the roots are tightly bound to or around the root ball, tease them free with your fingers on the sides and bottom. This may seem dramatic, but do it. It is for this reason that I pre-fer young bare root trees. Healthy young roots that have not been cramped or cut off will produce the healthiest and best anchored trees. Ironically folks go for the larger tree at the nursery, thinking it is the healthiest and strongest, or they go for the end-of-year-sale trees that have spent the extra season growing in the pots. These trees will look good for a few years after planting but then most likely will begin to have stress issues and become sus-ceptible to disease and drought.

Note that I do not recommend amending the planting hole with compost, fertilizer, or added organic matter of any kind. It is best to top dress and feed down. If you have cre-ated the "patch," you are set for top dressing and mulch. Don't worry if a little composted top soil gets down in the hole while planting, it's all good.

With the tree firmly planted, I pull the sheet mulch back in close to, but not touching, the tree trunk. Next, I water deeply to settle any air holes. That will be the last time I have to think of watering the tree as long as I've gone with the deluxe sheet mulch. The patch can now trap the flow of water moving across the landscape, a lot like a big sponge, and hold it where you are planting. In essence, you are creating a place to store and capture energy.

To help control vermin intruders, I make a tube of hardware cloth about a foot high, leaving a good inch of flex around the trunk. For larger vermin (deer, feral hippies, etc.), I fence with six-foot wire-welded fencing.

Notes: Bare root trees are catalog-ordered and come without soil while still dormant. It is usually the best way to get unique and affordable varieties. See the "Uncommon Fruits" chapter for recommended fruits and nurseries. Ringing the patch with daffodils and aromatic herbs will help deter deer. But if deer are a big issue, fencing or buckshot is the best solution.

Building the Guild: Companion Plants for the Patch

Permaculturists call groups of perennial companions "guilds." Guilds are the essence of the food forest design and balance. The idea here is that you are designing and planting to help meet the fruit or nut tree's needs at the beginning. Combining four or more companion plants in the patch results in higher plant production, reduced pest and disease problems, and increased soil fertility. Compare that to you doing all that yourself: buying fertilizer and expensive organic products — which in the end will be exhaustive attempts at maintaining fertile Black Gold. They're nothing like what a groovy little perennial ecosystem will offer.

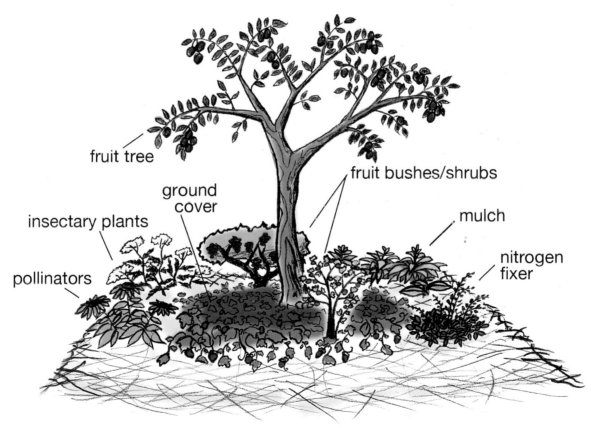

Perennial plant guild that helps balance the fruit tree's needs.

Model Patch

Whether it's with a new planting or a retrofit around an existing tree, the goal is a colorful assortment of different species with each playing a key role in the tree's health. My staple four companions around a tree are: comfrey, yarrow, echinacea, and blue wild indigo—the mulch, the insectary, the pollinator, and the nitrogen fixer, respectively. I delegate these all-star plants to each corner of the patch.

Comfrey

As the mulch, comfrey is a dynamic accumulator with a deep tap root that draws minerals and nutrients from the subsoil into its lovely, deep-green-lobed leaves. Chop and drop the comfrey three to four times during a growing season as mulch-in-place. There are many uses for this amazing plant other than the food forest; see the comfrey poultice recipe on page 69.

Yarrow

As the insectary — or beneficial insect plant — yarrow has amazing architecture that all kinds of beneficial critters love to live in and pollinate from. Aside from being beautiful, yarrow attracts parasitic wasps (not dangerous), lady bugs, and spiders, which help to balance pest populations. It is also another good mulch and fertilizer plant.

Echinacea

Echinacea, a.k.a., the pollinator, is the indigenous wonder that just won't stop flowering. It acts like a gas station to our winged allies who stop off to fuel up, munch a bug or two, and spread the love to your fruit trees. Echinacea is also a botanical healer.

Blue Wild Indigo

Then there's the wildest of the four all-stars: the blue wild indigo, the awesome nitrogen-fixer plant. She is the powerhouse of beauty and fertility as she simultaneously spikes her blue florescence into the sky and nitrogen nodules deep into the soil. Just don't chew the seeds, or she becomes a toxic beauty.

"Guild It and They Will Come"

It is important to note that other "volunteers" will gladly show up to the new oasis you have created. I welcome them as additions to the "chop and drop" mulch, which is just cut and left organic matter right where it's needed. Think of weeds as biomass, free and welcome mulch right where you need it. Muchas Gracias, Hierbas!

Guild it as you'd like — the more perennials you plug in, the more diversity and health your little food forest will have. I often add in gooseberries, lavenders, mints, ground covers like St. John's Wort, and strawberries to use the available space and light.

Note: Nitrogen fixers and dynamic accumulator plants such as lupines and comfrey can be planted right next to the tree; other companions, I spread around the patch's perimeter.

From Patches to Forest

If space allows, I will pace off 15 to 20 feet from the center of the patch to the center of another one, and then triangulate another, and so on. Keep making patches, and over time sheet mulch between; they will merge and create the dynamics of a

Other favorite companions

- Lead plant: nitrogen fixer; deer don't eat
- Lupine: nitrogen fixer; deer don't prefer
- Garlic, Egyptian Walking Onion: deer don't eat
- Horseradish: chop and drop mulch
- Rhubarb: chop and drop mulch; deer don't eat
- Nettle: mulch; compost; tea
- Black-Eyed Susan: Insectary
- Sweet Anne's Lace: great insectary
- Rocks and wood: pile them up as habitat

multi-layered food forest. When you've knitted together enough patches, you'll need to leave just enough space between them to push your harvest-loaded wheelbarrow through!

Note: The 15-20 feet relates to planting small-size fruit trees. Space 40 feet for nuts; 10 feet for shrubs.

Spaced patches will eventually grow together, forming a multi-layered food forest.

If putting in multiple patches, place your taller-growing trees to the north and the shorter trees to the south so that as the taller trees grow, they will not shade out the shorter ones once they mature. Also, consider placing the patches in a horseshoe shape that opens out to the south to create a suntrap and warm microclimate.

A Guild for Black Walnuts

Black Walnuts give off a natural chemical called jugalone that prevents many types of plants from growing near a mature tree. However, they do have some resilient friends that can grow near or inside the drip edge:

- Goumi bush
- Persimmon
- Paw paw
- Mulberry
- Currants
- Black raspberry
- Alpine strawberry
- Elderberry
- Goldenseal

Comfrey Poultice Recipe

The old monks used to call it knit bone and grew it in the monasteries for the bruised and broken wayward traveler. It has knitted and healed me more than a time or two, and I always have a poultice made and ready in the freezer, year round.

Scientifically, comfrey's healing power is from allantoin – a substance that speeds the production of new cells. But there seems to be much more in its magical healing abilities. Use the poultice for bruises, sprains, torn ligaments, fractured and broken bones, arthritis, sore muscles . . .

You will need:

- ❑ 3-4 large comfrey leaves
- ❑ ¼ cup water
- ❑ 1-2 cups of flour

Chop up the comfrey leaves into inch-size bits and place in a blender or food processor. Add just enough water to make a soupy paste. Scoop out into a bowl. Sprinkle on the flour a handful at a time and mix well until you have a guacamole-like thickness. Spread the poultice onto a cotton wash cloth ¼ inch thick, roll it up, and place in a zip lock bag for freezing, or apply directly using a small towel or saran wrap to hold the cloth in place.

Gooseberries, currants, blueberries, & raspberries from a stroll in the food forest.

Uncommon Fruits

"Fine fruit is the flower of commodities. It is the most perfect union of the useful and the beautiful that the earth knows. Trees full of soft foliage; blossoms fresh with spring bounty; and, finally, fruit, rich, bloom-dusted, melting, and luscious—such are the treasures of the orchard and garden, temptingly offered to every landholder in this bright and sunny, though temperate climate."—Andrew Jackson Downing, Bygone Ninja Horticulturist

Uncommonly delicious, uncommonly beautiful, uncommonly easy to grow . . . Yes, yes, yes. There is a world of fruit trees and bushes beyond the peach, cherry, and blueberry. These uncommon fruits fit perfectly in the front or back yard and require very little of you other than picking abundant harvests.

Culturally we have become accustomed to a handful of fruit trees and bushes that require an orchardist's hand and arsenal of sprays. But it's time for a revolution in the back yard. A revolution that brings us more ease in cultivation and rewards us with naturally healthy trees that drip with uncommon but delectable tastes.

The following fruits are just a sampling of the cornucopia that awaits to root in your landscape, titillate the senses, and fill the fruit bowl. Chosen for ease of care, beauty, and taste.

Persimmons are fantastic trees that produce exquisite fruit. Truly an edible landscape All-Star!

Persimmon, Asian & American

Diospyros kaki and Diospyros viginiana

- Zones: 6–10 for Asian, 4–10 for American
- Pollination: Variable, some need cross-pollination, some are self-fertile

Food of the Gods

The Greek for persimmon, Diospyros, translates roughly as "Food of the Gods," and rightly so, as eating a fully ripe persimmon can be a truly spiritual experience. The same can be said for eating an unripe one!

There are a few broad characteristics to get straight with persimmons. First, there are American and Asian persimmons. There is a big difference in the size of the mature tree—the American version averages 35 feet tall, and the Asian tops out around 15 feet. The American persimmon is still very much a woodland species, while the Asian persimmon has a rich history of cultivation. Funnily enough, most folks in America have never tried a persimmon let alone planted one, whereas in Asia this tree is found in nearly every yard within its growing range. The slow realization of how fantastic the persimmon is has translated into the American persimmon tree having far fewer cultivated varieties. In contrast, the Asian persimmon has over 2,000 cultivated varieties.

A second characteristic of persimmons is taste. The fruit is either astringent or non-astringent—basically, is it sour while firm or not? All the American persimmons are astringent until fully ripe . . . super ripe, to where the fruit looks ready for the compost bin. That's when it's exquisite! The Asian persimmon comes in both astringent and non-astringent varieties, meaning that some can be eaten while firm, while others must be left like the American versions to transform into heavenly jelly. To be safe, allow any persimmon to stay on the tree or counter until fully ripened to draw out the dynamic bouquet of flavors.

Zones

The United States Department of Agriculture (USDA) has created a map that outlines 11 zones across the country to mark the lowest average temperature in each region. Although approximate, it helps the gardener choose plants hardy to their region. The most up-to-date hardiness map can be found at the National Arbor Day Foundation website: www.arborday.org/media/zones.cfm.

Growing Your Persimmon

Like the Paw Paw tree, the Asian persimmon has a lush, tropical look, with large, drooping, flawless, green leaves that turn to gold and scarlet in the fall, leaving bright red and orange fruit hanging in the tree like ornaments. The Asian persimmon tree is a prime ornamental specimen that tops out at 15 feet tall. It requires very little care to stay beautiful and productive, even in the late, hot summers. The American persimmon is a stately, tall tree, with fascinating alligator bark. It is widely adaptable and cold-tolerant.

Persimmons are very easy, carefree trees to grow. They are bothered by few pests and affected by few diseases. They grow well in most soil types. For good fruiting, they need to receive full sun for most of the day. Buy young plants, either in deep pots or bare root, that have full undamaged roots. The Asian persimmon grows well in zones 7–10, where max cold temps bottom out at 0°F. Certain varieties, such as Jiro and Saijo, are successfully being grown and harvested in zone 6, where temps typically go no lower than -5°F. The varieties grown in the more northern zones tend to be astringent types, so the fruit from these varieties should be fully ripened before being enjoyed. The American persimmon is tough down to -25°F, zones 4–10.

Here in western Maryland - zone 7 - the Asian variety of Jiro has proven a good choice for beauty and heavy cropping. For colder regions I would recommend select American varieties of Meader, Early Golden, and Prok. There are also a handful of hybrid Asian and American persimmons that combine hardiness and flavor, zones 6–9: Nikita's Gift and Rosseyanka.

Pollination

Asian persimmons do not need another like tree for successful pollination, meaning you can plant one on its own and it will still bear fruit. The American cultivars need a male tree, except the Meader variety, which is partially self-fertile.

Fruit Drop

Premature fruit drop is common with Asian persimmons. There are a number of possible causes. One, the tree may naturally thin its heavy fruit set, sometimes dropping up to 75 percent of immature fruits. Two, too much shade can also drop a few. Three, too much fertilizer can be a cause. Often fruit drop is only in the juvenile stage, and the trees will balance with age.

Naked Trees!?

Don't fret if your newly planted persimmon tree remains bare of leaves while everything else in the landscape is leafing out. Persimmon trees tend to break dormancy late in the season and sometimes not until summer or even fall in areas with cool springs. Also important to note in regards to persimmon bare root trees: don't return them for their black roots as that's their natural color!

My Persimmon Story

Back in 2000, after picking the grape harvest in the foothills of the southern French Pyrenees, I left France for Italy, loaded with wine—cheap wine. French law allotted six liters of wine per day for pickers as part of their pay. I remember showing up in an Italian market town a bit bedraggled and very hungry. At a particularly colorful and fruitful grocers stand, I got stuck staring at rows upon rows of gorgeous fruits (which I mistook to be tomatoes), displayed in full Italian glory as they gleamed with smooth shiny skin in hues of orange and red. The grocer must have taken pity on my state and handed me one, gesturing and enthusiastically repeating "mangiare"! Oh, did my life ever change when I bit into that Diospyros—fruit of the gods! Three weeks of grueling grape picking, sleeping on the ground, and drinking cheap wine were suddenly a distant memory as I soared to the heavens on the flavors and texture of a persimmon. I felt like Marco Polo exploring a new and exotic world mingled with spice, honey, and apricot. When I came back to Earth and the smiling grocer—who must have seen this transformation before—I was a new man. I was truly in love!

Paw Paw

Asimina triloba

- Zones: 5–9
- Pollination: Needs cross pollination with another variety

Taste of the Tropics

Imagine a carefree, ornamental tree with a fruit filled with the creamy custard flavors of banana, mango, pineapple, and hints of vanilla. Meet the Paw Paw. Reputed to be the largest "native" fruit grown in North America, it is little-known to most Americans. The Paw Paw does not have a long storage life, nor does it have a thick skin needed for transporting. Otherwise, this exquisite fruit would be a well-known and favored fruit on the shelf. Ornamentally the Paw Paw stands alone with a perfect pyramid shape and long tropical-looking leaves that remain lush all summer long before giving a spectacular show of golden fall color. Paw Paws grow up to 25 feet tall but are easily maintained at 8 to 15 feet in height.

Growing the Paw Paw

To begin, buy grafted varieties grown in deep pots. The grafting will ensure consistency of growth and output, such as size, flavor, vigor, ripening time, and good yields, while the deep pots make sure the long tap root is not disturbed. Most bona fide mail order nurseries, like Raintree Nursery, will send you healthy grafted Paw Paws in 9-inch-deep pots along with your bare root trees.

Paw Paws planted by seed, called seedlings, do not promise to reproduce their parents' character. If you do buy young seedlings, you will need to keep them somewhat shaded for the first couple years of their life. You will not need to do so with mature grafted varieties.

Regardless of whether you use grafted varieties or seedlings, you should plant at least two trees. However, the more you plant, the better they will produce.

Full sized pair of paw paws planted together, 15 years old. Note the large unblemished leaves and pyramid shape of the tree.

In The Landscape

Though the Paw Paw grows wild as an understory plant, they fruit best in full sun. They make beautiful care-free front yard specimens with their pyramid shape, lush leaves, and brilliant golden fall foliage. Mulch well to keep soil cool and moist, much like the forest floor, and to help catch dropping fruit, which bruises easily.

The fruit can range from 3 to 6 inches long by 1 to 3 inches wide, about the size of a mango. The skin is smooth, green, and fragrant, and the flesh is creamy white to golden yellow with two rows of dark, flat seeds. Once ripe, Paw Paws only last for a few days—maybe a week in the fridge—so eat your fill and freeze the rest for making ice cream and smoothies. A good harvest can bring in a bushel per tree, about 30 pounds. Don't eat the skin or seeds to avoid possible bad reactions.

Two young grafted Paw Paws sitting on a swale with the nitrogen fixing Lead Plant between them, feeding steady fertilizer and mulch.

Notes & Tricks: Paw Paws start out slow-growing but build steam after a few years. Their flowers are these funky little purple numbers that hang like bells and have a smell that attracts flies, their main pollinator. Fortunately, the smell is not too shocking to the human nose. To help draw in more flies, I collect my dog's poop in buckets and place it under the trees. For a larger number of trees, get a bigger dog! To assure good fruit set, hand-pollinate them yourself by plucking off a flower with pollen and brushing it on the others.

The Paw Paw Guru — Neal Peterson

West Virginian Neal Peterson is the all-time Paw Paw hunter and breeder – a fruit fanatic's hero. Coming out of university in the mid-1970s with a head full of plant genetics, Neal stumbled into a Paw Paw patch and started a lifetime of Paw Paw cultivation and research. After many years of tracking down the old-named varieties long forgotten, Neal put his genetic wizardry to selection and new cultivars. His prize-winning varieties are named after U.S. rivers: Susquehanna, Shenandoah, Allegheny, Rappahannock. This is a far cry from the caveman's Paw Paw trees, which were seeded through the excrement of wooly mammoths. Look for Peterson's named cultivars through select nurseries via his site, www.petersonpawpaws.com

My Paw Paw Story

In September, during prime Paw Paw harvest season, I visited Jim Davis's Deep Run Paw Paw Orchard in Westminster, Maryland. Jim's one of the country's largest Paw Paw growers. After talking with Jim on the phone about our tropical food forests in Nicaragua and growing many of the Paw Paw's relatives, he invited me and fellow food forest magician Chris Shanks out to taste his Paw Paw patch and discuss funky fruits. Jim's orchard consists of about eight acres spread out on a rolling hilltop in full sun and ringed by woods. Under Jim's guidance, Chris and I explored row upon row of different varieties, picking and tasting the smooth, sweet, creamy, delicious pulp offered by this fascinating tree. Our biggest challenge was trying to keep track of the named varieties while fighting back the sugar belly. It was a touch of Heaven . . . the Willy Wonka Paw Paw Tour! (Kudos to Chris, who made it to the last row of goodness, trying every type of Paw Paw and grabbing a few for the road.)

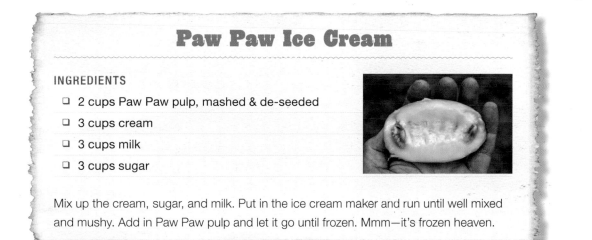

Paw Paw Ice Cream

INGREDIENTS

- ❑ 2 cups Paw Paw pulp, mashed & de-seeded
- ❑ 3 cups cream
- ❑ 3 cups milk
- ❑ 3 cups sugar

Mix up the cream, sugar, and milk. Put in the ice cream maker and run until well mixed and mushy. Add in Paw Paw pulp and let it go until frozen. Mmm—it's frozen heaven.

None of Jim's Paw Paw trees are seedlings. Rather, they are true clones—or grafts—of selected varieties. Jim prunes his trees in late winter down to about 8 feet tall. He does this by lopping the top off them while dormant, which they take surprisingly well and reshape nicely during the next growing season. Jim credits the good pollination of the trees to a diversity of insect habitat from the surrounding woods, as well as the sheer number of Paw Paws planted in a cluster. A few of Jim's favorite varieties are Shenandoah and NC-1. The latter, he adds, makes a supreme landscape specimen. Deep Run Paw Paw Orchard sells their fruit wholesale, mostly to specialty food stores (and quickly, before they spoil). Check Jim Davis' site out at www.deeprunpawpaws.com.

Hardy Kiwi

Actinidia arguta

- ○ Zones: 4–9
- ○ Pollination: Needs cross-pollination from male plant

The Bejeweled Vine

The hardy kiwi vine, a cousin of the fuzzy version, grows well in northern climates and is smooth and sweet, rather than hairy and tart. The hardy kiwi fruit is not that well-known commercially because of its short shelf life and wrinkled look when ripened. However, it is a fantastically flavored and productive fruit for the home grower.

Though emerald green on the inside like the fuzzy kiwi fruit, the hardy kiwi fruit looks quite different and produces smaller, inch-long, smooth-skinned fruits that grow in clusters and can be popped whole into the mouth like grapes. It is also a treat on the ornamental side with gorgeous shiny green leaves with red stems that stay lush throughout summer.

I am asked about how to grow hardy kiwis more than any other fruit. Folks are naturally curious when they see kiwi plants for sale at the box stores and grab one or two. They often take them home and plant along their chain link fence, not knowing what is soon to come. What a surprise once these vigorous vines get going . . . and cover their neighbor's fence, trees, and house! Think wisteria on steroids. On top of fantastic growth, each female plant can produce 100 pounds of fruit (if you've gotten your male and female ratio right). Amazing plant. Just don't plant it and forget about it!

Selecting and Trellising

To begin, determine if you have an adequate growing area that is able to support the hardy kiwi's vigorous growth and weight, approximately 200 square feet per plant. Then be sure you are selecting a male and a female plant, or at least one male per eight female plants (all plants sold in stores should be marked either male or female). The variety called "Issai" is an exception and is self-fertile, meaning it can be planted alone, but adding a male will still increase fruit size and yield.

As with grapes, the hardy kiwi vine makes a fruitful cover for a sturdy pergola or arbor. A minimum requirement is for trellising to be at least 6 feet off the ground, with room to spread laterally. I have seen this done in a variety of ways: a single wire between well-anchored posts, up a sturdy wall, as T-shaped trellises with multiple wires (like as a clothes line), or top-sturdy woody arbors. I have even witnessed wild ramblings on top of a carport—the key being to have strength, height, and space.

Training and Pruning

Hardy kiwi left on their own will twist and wrap and generally act crazy. This same vigor makes them fun to work with and learn from. From the moment of sprouting, train one shoot as your trunk. To do this, place a stake next to the shoot that reaches up to the height of your trellis (a piece of bamboo works great). Loosely tie the shoot to the stake and monitor it, assuring it grows straight, rather than curled around the stake. Remove any other side shoots along the trunk during the first growing season, spring and summer of the year it's planted.

Great shot by Mike McConkey of a hardy kiwi trained to a brick wall, back-dropping beds of currants and elderberry.

When it reaches the height of the trellis, which may be during the first or second season, prune off the growing tip to encourage lateral shoots to form. Select well-spaced shoots that line up with your trellis wires; these are called your cordons, or permanent arms of the plant. Tie these down as they run along the wires, and thin the side shoots that grow laterally from the cordons so that they are at least 6 inches apart; these will be your fruiting shoots. During the summer, trim these lateral shoots back, maintaining 15 to 18 inches in length to keep the vine in check and the energy toward fruit production. Also prune the fruiting shoots in late winter—while dormant—to just a few buds off the cordons. This may sound like a lot but is really a joy, and you learn to work with the vines very quickly as the kiwis grow fast.

Some kiwi growers may simply "whack back" the vines as they become unruly. A client of mine has a male/female pair of kiwis growing up her carport. These vines fruited partially thanks to her "whacking" it back to keep it the size of a hedge and preventing the vines from growing up and covering the roof. Though she knew nothing of

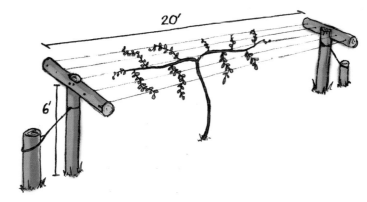

Pattern example of an intensely trained kiwi.

proper pruning for the kiwi, her "whacking back" approach actually stimulated new fruiting canes, allowed light to enter, and produced bud formation. So, if you already have a mature and/or wild kiwi (or you are on the way to having one), you can hedge it for partial fruiting or cut it back hard and re-train for full production.

Notes:

- Though the Hardy Kiwi is viable to -25°F, dormant plants are susceptible to cold-injury when young. To help avoid injury to the young vines and buds, do not plant the vines in low areas where frost collects, and wrap young vine trunks with burlap or tree wrap. Male vines are less hardy than females, and as a result of cold-injury, the vine may not pollinate for a season, resulting in poor or no fruit production, though the vine continues to grow.

- If the trunk does not grow strong the first season and reach the trellis height, cut it back by half in the late winter to stimulate new vigorous growth the following season. Likewise, prune back weak-growing cordons to strong buds to encourage healthier growth. Prune away shoots emerging from the trunk and shoots that are wrapping themselves around one another.

Harvest

Hardy kiwis have nearly double the sugar content of the fuzzy kiwi. That added sweetness means you have to eat them quickly once they are harvested. You will know they are ripe and ready when they soften, wrinkle, and pull off easily in your hand. Hardy kiwi can be picked while still firm in September and stored just above 32°F for about a month.

My Hardy Kiwi Story

My love affair with hardy kiwis hit its climax when I visited Mike McConkey's Edible Landscaping Nursery in Afton, Virginia, one ripe September day. Mike was part of bringing in the cultivated varieties of hardy kiwi in the 70's and has selected and grown out his favorites as a centerpiece of his nursery. Amongst his cornucopia of uncommon, funky, and delicious fruits is a hardy kiwi walk of fame. The kiwi walk starts with a trellised arbor covered in kiwi vine and hanging fruit, like the entrance to an Alice and Wonderland of Fruit, that leads you on to a vining hedge packed with hanging fruit where every lift of the vine reveals a stacked cluster of delectable kiwi ready for popping into your mouth. I was nearly crippled with sugar belly by the end of the row before I realized the other side was just as packed with hanging fruit! I took a deep breath and like any bona fide rare-fruit explorer, I munched on.

Note: Edible Landscaping Nursery, www.ediblelandscaping.com, has a diverse selection of potted plants that ship throughout the season. Tour and volunteer dates are posted on their website. I highly recommend going in the early fall/late summer when the place is dripping with uncommon fruits. And see if you can get Mike to sing one of his "fruitful" ballads.

Choice Varieties

FEMALES

- **Anna** - one of the most popular and widely sold varieties. Heavy yielder that produces large fruits up to ½ ounce with very sweet and flavorful fruit. Best in zones 5–7.
- **Dumbarton Oaks** - originally discovered in a public garden in the District of Columbia. Prized for sweet and delicious fruits that are slightly ribbed. Ripens early, about three weeks ahead of Anna. Zones 5–7, good in short summer regions.
- **Ken's Red** - fast and easy grower that bears good crops of large, sweet, smooth-skinned fruits that turn a purplish red as they ripen. Zones 6–9.
- **Issai** - a unique Japanese variety with excellent flavor, production, and appearance. Less vigorous than other varieties and partially self-pollinating, making it better suited for limited spaces. Cold hardy only to zone 6, minus -10°F.

RESOURCES

- "Growing Kiwi Fruit: A Pacific NW Extension Publication", Available through RainTree Nursery
- "Uncommon Fruits" by Lee Reich
- Hartmann's Plant Company has a good selection of very affordable kiwi and other unique small fruits. www.hartmannsplantcompany.com

Mulberry

Morus species

- Zones: 5–8
- Pollination: Self pollinating

King of Fruits

The selected, grafted mulberry is one of my all-time favorite fruits. Unfortunately, other than the persimmon, I don't know a fruit so misunderstood and underappreciated, relegated to the edge of popularity by weedy varieties. Fortunately, fruit explorers have selected and grafted choice selections amongst the "weeds", chosen for full aromas and balanced sweet/tart flavors that rival the best of berries.

Chances are you have only sampled wild bird-sown varieties which, while sweet and abundant, strike little resemblance to coveted "Black Persian" or "Shangri La" varieties that are as exotic in flavor as name. The mulberry fruit resembles a plump blackberry and comes in a range of colors; white, red, lavender, dark purple, and black. Their flavors range from insipidly sweet to cloyingly tart.

The Berry Tree

The mulberry tree has a wide growing range covering most of the U.S., growing an average of 35 feet tall, although easily maintained at 15 feet. Mulberries also have a wide range and adaptability for adverse soil conditions, including thin, gravely soil, rocky slopes, dry, wet, or alkaline soils, and other difficult areas. They also tolerate salt spray and produce fruit reliably in exposed areas and frost pockets, making them a very easy and successful tree to grow—proved by their weedy nature in the most inhospitable places. But one of the most amazing features of the mulberry is its ability to fruit in considerable shade as an edge species under larger trees. The only place mulberries aren't suited is near drives, walkways, or porches where fallen fruits will stain and track indoors.

The weeping mulberry variety makes a great children's fort that offers both shelter and food!

The mulberry's diversity of range is owed to there being three species; red, white, and black (rubra, alba, and nigra). The red and white species are the ones we are most familiar with and grow just about anywhere within their range (to -20°F). But the black beauty from western Asia and more moderate climes (to 0°F) is less known but renowned for its balance of flavor and stature. While the red and white mulberries grow generally to 35 to 50 feet and live up to 75 years, the black species tops out at 30 feet but often grows no taller than a bush and lives up to 300 years. All species are easily pruned to preferred height. Mulberry leaves have a unique tropical look and beautifully arching branches that can be showy as accent plants. On the larger landscape mulberries can be grouped together for wildlife habitat or planted as a screen or hedge.

Sweet Choices

Mulberries begin bearing in early summer with some varieties lasting until early fall. As testament to their superior flavor you will notice the birds swinging away from your berry bushes to happily sit in the mulberry tree, which easily produces enough fruit for all.

All three species have wonderful variety selections, but don't be surprised that the fruit color doesn't always line up with the species color; they are named for the color of their buds, not fruit. Black mulberries are only hardy to zones 7–10, while most white and red varieties are good in zones 5–8.

OF MENTIONABLE NOTE:

- **Illinois Everbearing** - White x Red hybrid - a fantastic selection that is very productive and hardy (-30 F). Black, sweet, almost seedless fruits 1½ inch long that bear from June through early fall. Good choice for northern climates, zones 4–9.

- **Wellington** - White x Red hybrid - A heavy cropper with sweet black fruits that bear over an extended period, another good northern variety, zones 5–9.

- **Black Persian** - Black - The Persian mulberry is a large purple/black berry that is excellent for fresh eating and making wine. Tends to grow as a bush. Zones 9–11, possibly to zone 7 once mature, if protected when young and most frost sensitive.

- **Kokusa Korean** - Black sub-species - is a fast growing mulberry from Korea that produces large 2-inch, high quality, firm fruits. Very hardy, zones 5–9. Fast producer from planting.

* Best way to harvest mulberries is to lay a large sheet or tarp under the tree and shake the fruit loose—easiest pickin' you've ever done. Mulberries are also very tasty dried and great in a trail mix. If you have chickens, place part of the tree to hang over the coop, and they'll be in heaven.

Mulberry Pie

Mulberries make my favorite berry pie. It is perfectly sweet all on its own, no sugar added, and is the easiest of all pies to make. Even wild varieties make a tasty pie. De-stemming is up to you, I find it tedious work and find no flavor difference leaving them on. It is mostly a visual thing. If you do remove the stems, I recommend scissors, as plucking each one would take Zen patience. Adding sugar is up to you, but each time I do I realize it was overkill. This pie can be as simple as crust and berries and turn out exquisite.

INGREDIENTS

- ❑ 4 cups mulberries
- ❑ ¾ cup white sugar (optional)
- ❑ ¼ cup all-purpose flour
- ❑ 1 9-inch pie crust
- ❑ 2 Tbsp. butter

DIRECTIONS

1. Preheat oven to 400°F.
2. Mix berries, sugar, and flour in a large bowl. Spoon mixture into bottom pie crust. Dot with butter. Top with full or lattice crust.
3. Bake at 400°F for 15 minutes, then lower oven temperature to 350°F and bake for an additional 30 minutes or until top is nicely golden.
4. Slice and share with soon-to-be mulberry converts.

Jujube

Ziziphus jujuba

- Zones: 6–9
- Pollination: Partially self-fertile, best production with 2 varieties

The Chinese Date

How about a small, attractive tree that has no disease or insect problems, doesn't suffer loss from late frosts, is at its peak of beauty in the heat of summer, and has a fruit as delectable as the apple and date together? Enter the Jujube tree, as carefree an ornamental edible as you will meet.

The Jujube is a small elegant tree that grows up to 25 feet tall, boasting immaculate green shiny leaves on pendulous branches that turn golden yellow in the fall, and attractive gray bark for year round beauty. But don't let their luscious looks fool you, as the Jujube tree will thrive under the harshest conditions.

The Jujube is a sure-fire recommendation for the low maintenance landscape with poor, compacted soil—which I think describes most of suburbia. This is a tree you can stick in the lawn and forget about the care notes. Plant a Jujube and you will be rewarded with a healthy, beautiful specimen that droops with sweet shiny fruit.

Lowdown on the Ziziphus

The fruit is the size of an apricot with a smooth skin that changes from light green to a handsome mahogany red as it ripens. Just as the fruit turns mahogany, it has a delightfully crisp, juicy flesh that is sweet like apples with hints of caramel and almond. Left to ripen longer on the tree, the fruit starts to wrinkle and concentrate its sugars and richness of flavors, earning its name as the Chinese Date.

Hardy to at least -10°F the Jujube can take almost any amount of summer heat and has best fruit set and flavor in hot summer areas. It takes full sun and is drought-tolerant. Branches are often contorted with a natural drooping habit, bowing beautifully when laden with fruit. Some varieties tend to produce suckers, so place where you can mow around or easily access to prune.

Notes: The Jujube produces some deciduous growth, so do not worry if some branchlets die off. Avoid cultivating the soil around the tree base to reduce stimulating root shoots.

Coveted Varieties

Flowers of the jujube can bloom sporadically throughout summer, staggering harvests from late summer into fall. Most varieties of Jujube trees only grow to about 15 feet in height, some boasting inch-long thorns (natural deer fencing), and some more prone to suckering than others. Here are a few favorites to consider:

- **Li** - one of the most popular varieties for its large, sweet fruit—about the size and shape of an egg—which can be eaten while still green. Nearly seedless. Best eaten fresh.
- **Lang** - pear-shaped fruit on an upright, almost thornless tree. Ripens just after Li but is best after fully red and ripe or dried for a caramel flavor.
- **Sherwood** - has a narrow weeping habit with large apple-flavored fruit. Few thorns, it is a good choice for long hot summers. A favorite for fresh eating.
- **Sugar Cane** - lives up to its name, with sugar sweet fruit that is well protected with spiny branches. A good choice for landscapes with deer pressure.

*Jujube candy is fashioned after the original candied jujube fruit that has a concentration of 75 percent sugar! Not that corn syrup crap.

RESOURCES

- Edible Landscaping in Virginia has a good selection and years of research behind their varieties of Jujube. www.ediblelandscaping.com
- Hidden Springs in Tennessee has a unique collection of fruits and Jujube. www.hiddenspringsnursery.com

Cider Apples & Perry Pears

Malus & Prunus species

- Zones: 4–9
- Pollination: Cross pollination needs 2 different varieties

Old Scrumpy

I rarely recommend planting apples to new home orchardists because of the intense care needed to stay disease-free, but my weakness for a good cider has me writing about them anyway.

Apples and pears are amazingly productive, so productive most folks just leave the fruit lying on the ground. The cure to this is planting cider apple and perry pear varieties, buying a press, and filling the jugs.

The trick to making good cider is starting with the right apple or pear. Most ciders these days are made with dessert apples, which is like making hot sauce with a bell pepper. A good cider wants complexity that balances sugar, tannin, acid, and aromatic oils, which is not your average table apple or pear tree. A few old heirloom apple varieties such as Kingston Black or Golden Russet make a balanced cider all on their own, but most hard cider makers blend varieties for the right zing.

Selection & Trellising

The best all-around apple I know for ease of growing, eating, storing, disease resistance, and cider is the Arkansas Black. A first runner up and pollinator is the variety Jonathan, which is a tart apple for cider or cooking.

Most perry pear varieties are old European ones like Hendre Huffcap and Barnet. Perry pears are reputedly named for Sir Geoffrey Perry, one of King Henry VIII's favorite cider makers—who must have added the right zing to keep his head.

For optimal health, plant pears and apples where there is good air flow and drainage, keep them well mulched and pruned. A favorite edible landscape design for apples and

Espalier fruit fence. Multi-grafted apple on left and pear on right.

pears to maximize space, air, and light is to espalier them. Espalier is a trellising technique for growing certain trees and bushes flat against walls or as stand-alone fruit fences. Developed in the Middle Ages within and along interior castle walls to help the population withstand sieges, it remains a functional design in today's urban and suburban landscape where space is tight and there is still a siege of fresh fruit.

The espalier fruit fence pictured here is used as a living wall to help enclose an outdoor eating area. The trellis is made of rot-resistant black locust posts centered in a bed 3 feet wide by 12 feet long. Two wires run at 2 and 4 feet high and support four branches on each tree. Each of the four arms of the apple on the left is grafted with a different variety, and the pear on the right also has four different pear varieties (ninja grafting), making cross pollination a breeze and offering 8 different fruit varieties in a 12-foot space. Production on an espalier can be heavy if the tree has ample light, good air flow, and reduced branching. With maturity, the trellis is phased out, and the thickened arms of the espalier hold their own form.

Many nurseries now sell pre-grafted and trained espalier trees that a trellis can be built to match or simply placed against a wall with a wire trellis system. The most common trees to espalier are apple, pear, cherry, and quince. Of them all, I find the pears to adapt best. Winter and summer pruning are needed. A good resource to learn more about training espaliers is the American Horticultural Society's "Pruning & Training Manual."

RESOURCES

- "The Apple Grower, A Guide for the Organic Orchardist" by Michael Phillips book & DVD. A great resource on holistic orcharding that goes far beyond apples.
- Raintree Nursery sells perry pears, cider apples and espalier trees. www.raintreenursery.com
- Maplevalleyorchards.com and treesofantiquity.com sell a plethora of cider apple varieties.
- "Craft Cider Making" by Andrew Lea

Goumi

Elaeagnus multiflora

- Zones: 4–9
- Pollination: Partially self-fertile, better yields with 2 varieties

Shimmering Beauty

The Goumi bush is possibly my favorite edible landscape All-Star. It checks off on beauty, ease of care, tasty fruit, and tolerance of a wide range of soils, making it a diamond even in the rough. Goumi is sometimes called cherry silverberry, a well-suited name for the small, juicy, sweet, tart, cherry-red fruits speckled with silver dots and shimmering silvery green foliage. This pretty bush tops out at about 6 feet wide and high on select varieties, blooming with cream colored flowers that fill the air with exquisite fragrance followed by abundant crops within a year or two of planting. Goumi bears fruit in June here in Maryland. I'm told Goumi fruits are excellent made into pies, jellies, and sauces, but I've never gotten past just stuffing them in my mouth by the handfuls.

Growing & Selecting

Goumi tolerates a wide range of soils and site conditions: dry, salty, low fertility, alkaline soils. It adapts to partial shade and even grows well with black walnuts. Goumi will grow just about anywhere except for where it stays wet. That means it's easy to grow and will thrive even with neglect. Part of its secret for being so versatile is that it's a nitrogen-fixer, meaning it has a relationship with beneficial bacteria on its roots to feed itself and surrounding plants. To top its rating as an All-Star, it is not favored by deer, though the chickens do bee-line for the bushes when hanging with fruit.

Young Red Scarlet is already loaded with tasty gems.

There are a few select cultivars, thanks to breeding programs at the Kiev Botanic Garden, Ukraine. The front-runners are Sweet Scarlet and Red Gem, who are twins both valued for productivity and very flavorful fruit. The Sweet Scarlet, true to its name, is my wife's favorite; and the Red Gem, a tad tarter, is mine. Plant both to decide for yourself and assure good pollination.

Stopping at just two will be hard. Fortunately the Goumi is easy to propagate and comes relatively close to its parent from seed. Seeds need cold stratification for one to two months before sowing and can take five-plus years to begin fruiting. A more surefire way to get a replica and quick fruiting is to clone with a stem cutting taken mid-summer. Take a 6-inch cutting of the current season's growth along with an inch of the older wood at its heel, dip in rooting hormone, pot in a well-draining mix, and maintain in a steady humidity to root. Start a Goumi forest!

RESOURCES
- Burnt Ridge Nursery is a good source for large bare-rooted selections. www.burntridgenursery.com

Sea Berry
Hippophae rhamnoides

- Zones: 3–7
- Pollination: Fruit-bearing females need cross pollination with male

The Medicinal Wonder

Also known as Sea Buckthorn, this compact regal shrub is widely grown and revered in Europe and Russia as one of the most medicinal fruits on the planet. Beyond its healthful fruits, it is a stand-out beauty in the landscape, growing upright to about 10 feet tall with gorgeous fruit-laden branches and narrow silver shimmering leaves.

Like the Goumi, it is widely adaptable to poor soil conditions and fixes its own nitrogen. Unlike the Goumi, you do not want to eat its berries out of hand, unless you really like sour. It's good to sweeten them up as a juice. Although sour, the Sea Berry is wonderfully flavored, reminiscent of oranges and passion fruit. Small oval fruits are born in late summer and fall as long cascading clusters of bright orange-yellow berries that create a striking contrast to the shrub's silvery green leaves. A stunning feature in the edible landscape.

The Sea Berry has been used for thousands of years in Eastern Asia and Russia as a cure-all, treating all sorts of health issues and illnesses. A super fruit with an impressive nutritional profile, Sea Berry boasts 14 essential vitamins, super-charged anti-oxidants, anti-inflammatory properties, omega's 3, 6, 7, and 9, and hundreds of other nutrients. The berries' oil is a healer for any kind of skin damage and is renowned for supporting mucous and tissue membranes. It is beginning to pop up in high-end organic skin products like Weleda as a "beauty berry" that nourishes skin and body tissue from the inside-out. Your all-in-one fruit supplement!

In the Landscape

The Sea Berry is adapted just about everywhere in its regional range, even in sand. It's perfect for that ignored part of the landscape that has poor dry soils, high or low pH, and where nothing else wants to thrive or the deer munch everything down to the ground. The buckthorn version of the name is well earned, as many varieties have gnarly 1-inch thorns that keep deer and mooches at bay. Granted this does make harvesting a challenge and is why some cultures just lop off the branches and freeze them to make the berries fall off easily. Those thorns can also make the sea buckthorn a veritable barrier as a living fence to keep varmints and zombies at bay. Some varieties are prone to sending up suckers that can be easily pruned away or left to help form a hedge. These characteristics also make the Sea Berry a good candidate for soil erosion control and land reclamation projects.

Favored Varieties

The Russians have led the selection and propagation of Sea Berry, focusing on varieties that are adapted to long, cold winters. The Germans have led the way with varieties suited for continental and coastal climates. They are all bred for high quality fruit, flavor, and ease of harvest.

THE RUSSIANS

- **Garden's Gift** - bred at Moscow State University to produce copious amounts of large, deep orange, and very aromatic fruit. Pretty shrub with pendulous branches.
- **Russian Orange** - another beautiful producer of flavorful orange berries and less thorny than most varieties.

THE GERMANS

- **Leikora** - heavy fruiter of tart orange berries that hang on the plant until heavy frosts. Very ornamental shrub that grows to about 10 feet tall. Laden branches make beautiful additions to floral displays.
- **Golden Sweet** - has an upright growth-habit and produces yellow-orange berries that come as close to sweet as a Sea Berry can. Good choice for making liquors and infusions. Can take longer than other varieties to begin bearing but well worth the wait.

RESOURCES

- Both Raintree and One Green World have excellent selections of Sea Berry.
- Ben Falk's book "The Resilient Farm and Homestead" has great information on growing, using and propagating Sea Berries.

Our feathered friends also love the gooseberry! Bushes are easily covered with bird netting to assure you get some, too.

Gooseberries & Currants

Ribes spp.

- Zones: 3–8
- Pollination: Self-fertile, no pollinator needed

Gooseberry

I plant more gooseberries than any other fruit in my food forest gardens. It has a perfect size as a small bush and is partially shade-tolerant, giving it versatility hard to match. And what flavor-packed jewels it produces—hanging all along its arms, every color of the rainbow. A royal fruit in any landscape.

Gooseberries hail from northern climates and have a rich history of breeding and use in European culture; just ask an older friend from that part of the world about gooseberries, and you will see their eyes light up in reminisce of bygone gooseberry pies and jams. The best of gooseberry selections have a juicy aromatic pulp with a sprightly sweet sour flavor that puts grapes to shame. The worst of them will make you pucker and twist. Fortunately, its European popularity has led to many sweet cultivars that are easily and inexpensively available from bare root mail order nurseries. A few recommended varieties for flavor and disease resistance are Invicta, Pixwell, Poorman, and Hinnomaki Red.

The gooseberry bush has a diversity of growing habits, but most contain themselves in an orb shape approximately 3 to 5 feet tall and round. It has arching arms that hang heavy with fruit and attractive lobed leaves. Most gooseberries protect their bounty and beauty with an army of thorns, just enough to keep the deer from nosing too far down. Fruiting follows strawberries in late June/early July.

Gooseberries can be trellised as fans in urban spaces quite easily, creating a unique and fruitful curiosity.

Though cold-hardy and shade-tolerant (up to 40 percent shade), I find they like open sun and good airflow so long as they are well-mulched underneath. Care is simple and is based on good mulching and pruning to maintain good air flow and new fruiting wood.

Currants

Currants are a stately bush of upright canes, attractive leaves, and fruits like dangling pearls that are beauties in any edible landscape. Another European and Russian favorite that bursts with flavor and tremendous aroma, though not for the lighthearted as they are quite tart and acidic. These qualities make them ideal for jam and winemaking.

Similar in size to the gooseberry but thornless and erect in growth, usually between 3 and 5 feet, they blend in nicely at the shrub layer around trees, foundation plantings, and next to evergreens. I plant them between fruit trees where they get just enough light to fruit (6 hours) and stay cool in our hot Maryland summers. There are black, red, white, and pink types of currants that go from very tart to sweet, respectively. Aside from their packed flavor, the currant boasts 5 times the vitamin C of oranges by weight, and twice the potassium of bananas and antioxidants of blueberries.

Care is simple, as for gooseberries: keep the ground well-mulched and prune to keep the air flow. A few recommendable varieties of the black currants—Ben Sarek and Swedish Black—and of the red currants: Red Lake, and Jonkheer Van Tets. Of the white and pink currants: Primus and Blanca White, and Pink Champaign. Raintree Nursery has a fine and extensive list of currants to choose from for the home gardener.

Jostaberry

The Jostaberry is a cross between a gooseberry and black currant that captures the best of both in a thornless bush with sweet berries. The Jostaberry has a more vigorous growth, easily reaching over 6 feet and ranging wildly. If you have the space, this wild child is worth every inch.

Pruning Gooseberries & Currants

It's important to remember that gooseberries and currants produce fruit on one- , two- , and three-year-old wood.

- Prune gooseberries and currants when the plants are dormant in late winter or early spring.
- After the first year of growth, remove all but 7 or 8 of the most vigorous shoots.
- At the end of the second growing season, leave the 4 best one-year-old shoots and up to 4 two-year-old canes.
- At the end of the third year, prune so that approximately 4 canes of each age remain.
- Fourth year and onward, the oldest set of canes should be pruned, allowing the new canes to grow.
- Always remove any diseased or broken branches and any that lie along the ground.

This rhythm of pruning ensures that the plants remain productive. A strong, healthy, mature plant should have about 8 to 10 bearing canes, with younger canes eventually cycling out the oldest. This not only optimizes fruit production but keeps the bush breathing and helps prevents fungal disease.

Fruit Tree Care

Fruits can be the easiest part of your landscape to manage. By selecting easy-to-grow varieties and setting up the soil as we covered in the Food Forests chapter, even the first-time grower will have success.

Everyone, even the beginner, has their own style as they garden, and many beautiful gardens have no rhyme or reason to their success other than the gardener's magic and relation to place and plants. The only way to truly learn gardening is to go for it; be observant of what worked or what didn't and imitate natural patterns as best as possible. Therefore the following care notes are to be carried lightly with you as you enter the landscape where intuition and reflection are your best guides.

Pruning and Shaping

Fruit trees that have been potted or transplanted often need continued care and support in balancing their form, especially for good fruit production. Fortunately, pruning is far more simple than most folks think, especially when started with early shaping. Rather than give an academic account of the various pruning styles and approaches, I hope to impart here a sense of what to do as you approach your tree or bush and how to arm yourself with the proper pruning gear.

The first thing to do is acquire the right tools and assure that they are properly sharpened. Please do not grab those old, dull loppers hiding in your shed, intending to prune anything beloved. For most pruning and shaping needs I use only two tools; a hand pruner and a folding pruning saw. I also keep a pocket sharpener on hand to keep the blades of the hand pruner sharp, assuring clean cuts.

Hand pruners are ideal for cutting anything smaller than the size of your index finger. Just about any hand pruner you purchase will do the job, as long as they are "bypass," meaning the two blades work like scissors. I also recommend using the little holster most pruners come with that clips to the belt or waistband, leaving your hands free between cuts. To sharpen the hand pruner blades, I use a nifty little gadget by Smith's Sharpeners that sharpens pruners up in a jiffy.

Shaping Up

The term "shaping" is used when talking about directing the plant's form, usually when young. "Pruning" refers to thinning and opening up a mature tree or bush. The two terms often overlap.

The folding pruning saw works for cutting branches up to 6 inches thick and efficiently replacing loppers. Beyond that, consider busting out the chainsaw. Any folding pruning saw you purchase will do, as long as the blade can be replaced easily, since they cannot be sharpened. Felco makes good pruning tools and replacement blades.

Approaching the Tree

Where shaping and pruning is involved, there is an old adage that states, "A bird should be able to fly through the tree." If you make this your mantra, pruning is going to be a breeze. The saying is designed to teach two of the most important concepts of healthy fruit tree shaping: air flow and light. Air flow allows the tree or bush to "breathe" and reduces the dank, stagnant conditions that funky fungi, bacteria, and viruses thrive in. Allowing proper light through the tree also reduces these conditions, while supporting the development of fruit buds, which are most often found on the inside branches.

WHAT TO CUT

When deciding which branches to cut, it is important to first stand back and observe the tree. To begin:

1. Prune out any branches that are growing across or rubbing against other branches.

2. Prune branches that are growing downward or toward the center of the tree.

3. Prune out any branches that appear diseased or broken.

4. Prune out competing central leaders and sprouts that are clogging the tree's center.

HOW TO CUT

How the branches are cut is simple but important to do correctly to maintain the overall health of the tree. The main rule is to never make the cut so close that the trunk is damaged or so far away you leave a big nub that rots.

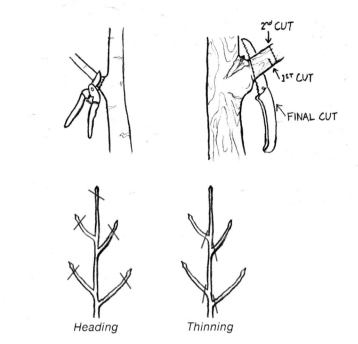

Heading   Thinning

1. When pruning a small branch, make a clean cut 1 inch from the body of the tree at a slight angle (approximately 30 degrees) away from the trunk.

2. For large branches make a cut on the underside forward from the final top cut, and remove bulk of branch and weight. Lastly make a third cut to cleanly remove the stub. This will prevent the bark from stripping downward on the trunk.

3. Use thinning cuts all the way back at the branch base. A heading cut farther out on the branch creates a hedging effect and further clogs the tree.

WHEN TO CUT

Remember that pruning trees, or shaping, is best done in the late winter before sap rises. Prune water shoots and shoots from the trunk base throughout the year.

Shaping the Young

If you are starting out with a young tree that is one to two years old, you can shape its lifelong structure with just a few snips. Most bare root trees ordered from catalogs arrive at about two years old and 3 to 4 feet tall. Trees sometimes arrive as "whips," which mean they have no branches. However, most often they already have two or three small side branches, which you may or may not choose to keep, depending on their orientation. Though these little branches look insignificant, they will eventually become thick branches that will be the main frame of the tree. These main frame branches are called the tree's "scaffold," and that's what we want to shape.

Whether you start with a bare root tree or a more developed tree, they usually come with a few existing branches, often coming off the trunk at 2 or 3 feet high. If there are three or four branches well-spaced around the tree at the same height, you are set. If you have more than four branches at the same height, prune the extras so that the remaining three or four branches are well spaced in opposite directions, like the four points of

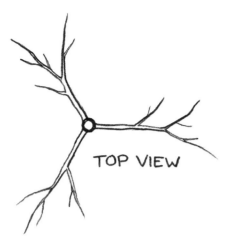

TOP VIEW

a compass. It's helpful to lean over the tree and look down at the branches like hands on a clock to best see their radial spread.

Depending on the type of tree, you may only want to keep these three or four spread scaffolds and discourage any further vertical growth on the trunk. This training is called the open vase and resembles an inverted umbrella. Or, you can allow the trunk to continue up and branch again in another well-spaced orientation of three or four branches; this shaping is called a central leader. Do not fret over which is best but rather how you would like the tree to grow in your landscape. The concepts for both styles focus on opening the tree for air and light flow.

Note: If you are individually fencing your trees due to deer browsing, snip the side branches off clean at the trunk and allow the leader to grow up higher. When it reaches about 5 feet high, snip it above a bud to force branching at that height, then select three or four well-spaced branches. This does make your fruit higher to reach but allows strong, healthy branches to form instead of bent and crippled ones caught in the fencing.

The Older Tree

The mature fruit tree that has never been pruned or shaped is usually a wild jungle of branches: branches crisscrossing, crowded in the middle, angled downward, broken, and hanging. This is where you usually stand staring in wonder at where to begin.

Though the temptation to whip the tree into shape all at one time is hard to resist, it is best to pace its return to glory gradually by removing a maximum of 25 percent of the tree's mass each year. An unruly, full-sized tree can take up to three years to work back into shape and health.

Note: Many fruit trees, especially apples, respond to intense pruning by sending up water sprouts, which are soft vertical shoots. These should be pinched or nipped off throughout the growing season; otherwise, they will thicken and become unwanted branches.

Is It Worth It?

Consider whether the older tree is strong enough to handle intense pruning. Is it worth the pruning process, versus cutting it down and replanting another tree? If the latter, be sure to choose a tree better suited to the site, one that can be shaped and pruned from the beginning. Replanting often results in getting a harvest in the same amount of time as bringing back an older, overgrown, existing tree.

- Do not fertilize during the years of intense pruning, as pruning already stimulates new growth.
- Combining pruning with sheet mulching out to the drip edge (where the branches reach) will double the tree's response time and return to health. See the Food Forest chapter for sheet-mulching instructions.
- Heavy pruning can reduce or eliminate harvests for the year but will eventually help the tree regulate its bearing to produce fruit every year.

Painting young trees and newly exposed branches with a homemade tree paint can help them deal with winter sun scald and sunburn. Yes, exposed branches and trunks can get sunburned. Think of tree painting as sunscreen.

(For bush fruit shaping and pruning see Gooseberries & Currants on page 94.)

Tree Paint

Heavily pruned trees and young tree trunks are sensitive to summer sunburn and winter sun scald, respectively. To protect recently exposed branches and young trunks, I use and recommend a home-made reflective "tree paint." The Cornell Extension agent who taught me about pruning temperate trees said to simply mix a 1:1 ratio of water and indoor white latex paint. Since this is basically a lime wash, the latex could be traded out with a hydrated lime powder or a milk-based paint.

For young trunks, regardless of whether you have pruned them or not, paint all the way up the trunk and into the main branches. This white layer helps reflect the winter sun that heats up the south-west side of a tree's bark during the day, causing it to expand. Then, during the night, that same bark contracts when it gets cold or freezes. This expansion and contraction creates fissures along the bark, like cuts on the skin, which enlarge with age and become entryways for disease and insects. To make this mix more multifunctional, add in finely sifted compost as a microbial inoculant, dried blood meal

Tree paint on young trunk. Also note the hardware cloth around base to deter chewing critters.

as fertilizer and deer repellent, diatomaceous earth to help deter pest larvae, and kaolin clay to bolster the "sunscreen" and smother overwintering insect eggs. For trees newly exposed from heavy pruning, paint the tops of the remaining branches exposed to the sun.

Kaolin Clay

Kaolin is a very fine powered clay used on plants to deter crawling insects. If applied early in the season, before critters like stink bugs and Japanese beetles get crawling, it is an effective protectant. By coating the leaves of plants with the fine clay as a spray, you create an unwelcome surface to crawling bugs—just imagine your eye and ear openings filled with irritating clay particles and your reproductive parts literally clogged . . . surely you'd want to boogie from such a place. By deterring many crawling insects like the curculio and codling moth from landing and laying larvae, the cycles of infestation can be broken for seasons to come, benefiting your plants in the short and long term. Kaolin clay is just as effective on your fruit trees as on your tomatoes and ornamentals. Be sure to apply three good coats at the early stages of the season. Don't worry about impeding sunlight and photosynthesis, as the clay actually helps plants to reduce sunburn and balance light intake. Our beneficial flying allies are not negatively affected by the clay as they land and launch with ease. The best resource to learn more about Kaolin clay is Michael Phillips' book "The Apple Grower: A Guide for the Organic Orchardist."

Guerilla Grafting, Tree Shaping, and Fruit Cocktails

"Guerilla Grafting" refers to reworking, or grafting, a new variety onto an existing tree; i.e., putting a Bartlett Pear on an ornamental street tree pear. It is a way to switch the fruit variety on an older tree that needs improving or to make an ornamental tree of the same type become fruitful. It does not require setting up a nursery; there's no need to mess with seeds or potting soil; and one does not even need to own land to propagate fabulous fruits in the landscapes around us. You do not need to be a Ninja to graft. It is not a complicated matter or an advanced horticultural skill.

Simply put, "grafted" means that two varieties of the same fruit have been grown together for strength and flavor, such as a crab apple and a Golden Delicious. The crab apple provides a strong root structure that adapts to tough conditions, while the Golden Delicious is grafted atop as if on piggyback, tapping into those resilient roots while popping off its sweet golden apples. The Golden Delicious grown on its own roots would be a weak tree inclined to disease and limited soil conditions—a princess in the wild, if you will—but once grafted onto a hardy crab apple, the Golden Delicious is lifted free of its own root structure and fed all it needs to flourish and produce. Much like the farmer's son marrying the princess. We call this marriage "root stock and scion."

The root stock affects tree size, disease resistance, temperature, and soil adaptability, while the scion is a clone cutting that is guaranteed to produce the same fruit as the tree from which it was taken. Fruit trees purchased from the nursery come already grafted, even though they are only labeled Gala, Fuji, etc. The unnamed root stock is there with its only mention being the tree's size: dwarf, semi-dwarf, or standard.

How it Happens

The scion is a cutting from the branch tip of a selected cultivar about 8 inches long, with the thickness of a pencil. This cutting is a clone, meaning it has the exact same genetic makeup as the branch it came from, as compared to a seed taken from a fruit grown on the same branch, which would not have the exact same genetic makeup, since it has mixed genes from cross-pollination.

By gathering this scion cutting, the propagation of the exact same fruit is assured. These cuttings can be conveniently collected at the same time as when pruning occurs in the late winter. Healthy branch tips are snipped, wrapped in a damp paper towel or newspaper, sealed in a plastic zip lock bag, properly labeled, and placed in a refrigerator. These scions will remain in the fridge for approximately one month, until leaf break on the trees occurs. The scions are then shaped and joined to the root stock/existing tree to "heal" together and grow as one (more on this in a minute).

Most of us don't have a nursery full of root stock seedlings all lined up to graft scions on, but if you start looking out into the landscape, you will see lots you can graft onto. Already planted or wild-grown trees are great to graft on because they have established roots and have adjusted to their habitat. Examples of such trees include ornamental crab apples, plums, and pears in your yard or on your street, hawthorns, wild-grown American persimmons, wild apples along the road grown from someone chucking out an apple core—hell, even your neighbor's branch that is sticking through the fence are all game for grafting.

There's root stock everywhere! Somehow someone has thoughtfully established your root stock for you. Cut scion wood from good fruiting varieties, and graft away!

What's Compatible?

Generally speaking, only members of the same botanical family can be grafted together. Here are a few examples:

- European Pear /Ornamental Pear/Hawthorn/ Medlar/Quince
- Apple /Medlar/Crab Apple
- Peach/Nectarine/European Plum/ Almond/Ume/Apricot/Plumcot/Asian Plum/Ornamental Plum
- Sweet Cherry/Sour Cherry/Ornamental Cherry

How to Graft

No matter how guerilla you are, there are still a few rules to follow about grafting. The scion and root stock marriage is all about lining up the cambium, the lime green layer just

Scion cutting from heirloom apple.

Opening up the cambium layer on crabapple - the root stock.

Inserting the scion wood cutting into the root stock, lining up the cambium layers.

Crabapple reworked on all three main branches, waxed and taped.

Cleft graft of same sized scion and root stock.

Smaller diameter root stock and scion, waxed and wrapped.

under the bark. The cambium is the life blood of the tree, where water and sugar are flowing up and down like a big vein. Regardless of the size difference between the scion cutting and the root stock you are grafting onto, the cambiums need to line up.

With guerilla grafting and reworking older trees, you are usually grafting onto large branches and trunks with a little, pencil-sized scion. As seen in picture series, we place the scion to the edge of the branch or trunk where it can meet cambium with cambium. To keep it simple, we will discuss doing this with a cleft graft, one of many ways to make the scion wood and root stock fit together. Creating the cleft graft is easy. Make a wedge out of the scion by cutting the bottom inch of it at a diagonal, and make a cut in the root stock branch to receive the scion. I will often put three or more scion cuttings on a large branch or trunk to help assure that at least one of them takes. Once lined up and slid into place, the graft needs to be sealed to hold in moisture while the cambiums heal together. You can use a heavy duty petroleum jelly, beeswax or grafting wax as a sealant. If the union is not stable, you will also need to wrap it tight with electrical or grafting tape. For grafting smaller branches or seedling stems the same size as your scion wood cutting, cover the union with petroleum jelly or grafting wax and wrap tightly with electrical or grafting tape.

RESOURCES

- "The Grafter's Handbook" by R.J. Garrner
- A good source for uncommon fruit scion wood is England's Orchard & Maple Valley Orchards in Kentucky. www.nuttrees.net
- Raintree Nursery in Washington state sells limited species of bare root root stock. www.raintreenursery.com

Hugelkultur
MOUNDS OF FERTILITY

"Hugelkultur" roughly translates from German to mean "mound culture." It's an ancient practice of creating raised garden beds by covering wood with soil.

The buried wood acts like a sponge, capturing water and nutrients for later use by whatever you choose to plant. As it decomposes, the wood draws in beneficial fungi and quickly turns into rich soil. The results are astounding for such a simple process and creates the most amazing, fertile, and self-hydrating raised beds!

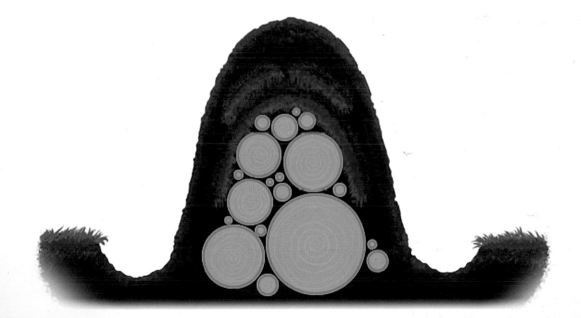

How It Works

A hugelkultur bed imitates a forest floor. Woody material falls, absorbs moisture, then decays, thus feeding the nutrient cycle and plants around it. By covering wood with sod, soil, and/or compost, you create a moist environment perfect for fungi to colonize. Fungi quickly begin to break the wood down into the most fantastic planting soil and stage the bed for worms and other soil builders. As the buried, decomposing wood breaks down, it gives off heat—as all compost does—and opens up tiny air pockets, creating optimal soil conditions for plants to thrive. (The nitrogen will be tied up in the wood decomposition for the first season, if it's new wood, but then the tables turn and the nutrients release like a flood).

What's Great About Hugelkultur

- Amazing Water Retention
- Warmer Soil
- Builds Soil Fertility
- Creates Micro-Climates
- Recycles Organic Matter On-site
- Less Bending Over!
- Cleans Your Yard up in Style

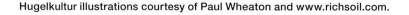

Hugelkultur illustrations courtesy of Paul Wheaton and www.richsoil.com.

Where and How?

Just by chucking some soil on top of a wood pile, you can turn inhospitable areas—compacted, wet, or dry—into thriving, growing systems. Hugelkultur beds can be built up with any size or age of wood, from branch trimmings to huge chunks of wood . . . even whole trees. The taller the pile (up to six feet), the better. Taller piles will hold more moisture in their decomposing, woody mass. A tall hugelkultur bed can also serve as an immediate barrier to road noise, unsavory neighbors, etc.

That said, even a 1- or 2-foot-high micro hugelkultur can take advantage of using smaller debris and become a fertile pile of sticks!

Building a Hugelkultur Bed

This is a simple, straightforward process:

1. Pick a site for your bed—an area at least 3 feet wide by 6 feet long. Ideally, you can site a hugel bed on contour or perpendicular to the slope to harvest rainwater runoff, adding to the bed's hydration and plantings downslope.

2. Gather your materials:
   - New or old wood of all sizes (avoid locust, walnut, cedars, and other trees that are slow to break down or contain tannins)
   - Sod, leaves, manure, kitchen compost
   - Top soil
   - Straw

3. Layer the woody debris, starting with the largest diameter on the bottom, becoming smaller as you rise up. Any height works, but the higher, the better to allow for longer moisture retention.

4. Stuff the gaps with upturned sod, leaves, compost, or manure.

5. Cover with at least two inches of top soil, then add straw as mulch. If the bed is tall, you may need to secure the straw by pinning it down with V-shaped twigs or by leaning branches against the pile.

Small-scale hugelkultur beds from prunings fit well in the raised bed garden. The hugel beds here show recently created mounds (top) and the same bed two years later (bottom), planted for chicken fodder at Harvey Ussery's homestead. www.themodernhomestead.us.

This hugelkultur bed was designed to capture a large volume of water coming downslope and hydrate a garden below. Excavated with a small Bobcat on contour and filled with storm-fallen poplar logs and brush. The sod was placed to one side and laid on top of the wood before layering on the soil. The bed was then edged with stone, covered with straw, and seeded with cow pea as a cover crop. This hugel bed now harvests a huge volume of rainwater runoff passively, both for itself and also for the raised bed garden (left). Win, win!

Sink It

Hugelkultur beds come in just about every style, fashion, and size. The simplest is a well-packed pile of wood debris laid directly on the ground, then covered with top soil and straw, as outlined above. This alone will work wonders, but sunken hugelkultur beds also have their benefits.

Build a sunken bed by excavating the width and length of the bed 1 to 2 feet deep, separating the excavated sod and soil for later reapplication. Lay the woody debris down in the excavated bed, then build up as described above. This approach has a stronger water-harvesting element, since it also acts as a swale if dug on contour (see Rainwater Harvesting chapter). A big benefit of excavating first is that it provides the sod and soil needed to cover the pile of wood.

You can create your own variation of a hugelbed; the concept is adaptable to your site, materials, and imagination. Be patient and you will be rewarded with the most amazing, fertile beds. Ninja move: if you have fresh, healthy wood cut while dormant you can inoculate the wood with oyster or shiitake strains before putting in the hugelkultur.

Planting the Hugelkultur

If the season allows it, sow a cover crop immediately after building the hugelkultur. I sow whatever I have on hand—clovers, cow peas, vetch. Remember that the first year, nitrogen will be tied up in the decomposition process of the wood, so be patient. After a full growing season, the hugel will have dropped in height by a third, and will have built up nutrient levels and moisture retention. At this point, you can continue with the cover crops for another season and/or begin to plant in other annuals and perennials.

A large hugel bed will hit its stride in the third year; smaller hugel beds will be ready as early as the second season.

Hugel bed in second season, beginning to plant perennials.

Berries seem to love hugel beds and make for a great picking height. I plant blueberries, lingonberries, raspberries, figs and hazel nuts, mixed in with rhubarb, comfrey, sage, Egyptian walking onions (the funky guys popping out in the picture at right) and black-eyed Susans that will all eventually turn into a fedge!

Try playing with the micro-climates on the hugel; i.e., plant cool-weather plants on the north or east side, and warm-loving ones on the south or west. You will be amazed at the growth and flavor. Hugel beds grow the tastiest fruits that can be used to create your own fine wines.

However you plant it, you will get great returns just for chucking some dirt on wood. Love it!

In building our circular round-wood timber-frame strawbale house, we did a little site-clearing for access and safety. Instead of hauling the wood offsite and setting up artificial erosion fences (which is the norm in house site construction), we piled it high and covered it with the soil from the foundation excavation. We recycled all the materials onsite into multiple hugelkultur beds that harvest all the rainwater runoff and erosion. We will now have fertile garden beds for planting when we move in.

How Hugelkultur Saves the World

Hugelkultur is a great way to recycle and capture the resources produced by the land. Ideally, all of the resources coming into or onto our sites are captured and stored, with water and organic matter being the most tangible. I often come across folks who are piling up branches and leaves by the roadside for pickup. That debris usually ends up in a landfill, where it breaks down slowly and definitely is not used to its full potential. This is an incredible loss to the site, as those branches and leaves can be easily transformed into great growing material.

Another great "waste" source is soil. It is not hard to find someone in the neighborhood digging up the earth for a variety of reasons. Often, those people are looking to get rid of the soil, which is a perfect opportunity for a hugelkulturist. For example, you can build a rain garden and hugelkultur at the same time, using the excavated soil and sod from the rain garden to cover the hugelkultur bed.

The Duke of Permaculture

Paul Wheaton is this superbly obnoxious guy out in Montana that has dedicated himself to building an empire of permaculture knowledge and resources, earning the title "Duke of Permaculture." He has more than 100 podcasts filled with humor, rant, and gems of insight for navigating the complexities of the permaculture world. His online forum is an encyclopedia of real-life knowledge and experience from a large and responsive community. www.Permies.com.

Stacking Functions

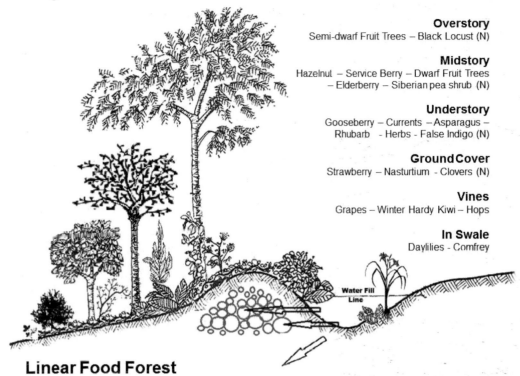

Overstory
Semi-dwarf Fruit Trees – Black Locust (N)

Midstory
Hazelnut – Service Berry – Dwarf Fruit Trees
– Elderberry – Siberian pea shrub (N)

Understory
Gooseberry – Currents – Asparagus –
Rhubarb - Herbs - False Indigo (N)

Ground Cover
Strawberry – Nasturtium - Clovers (N)

Vines
Grapes – Winter Hardy Kiwi – Hops

In Swale
Daylilies - Comfrey

Water Fill Line

Linear Food Forest
Perennial trees and plants located along the entire downhill side of the hugelkultured swales

This wonderfully illustrated hugelkultur and swale combo—modified by the fine folks at Midwest Permaculture from Bill Mollison's "Introduction to Permaculture"—stacks the functions of passive rainwater harvest, organic matter recycling, and food forest design. Ninja design at its best. Midwest Permaculture also has good videos on hugelkultur design at www.midwestpermaculture.com. Note: The (N) next to some of the listed species denotes them as nitrogen fixers.
Build a hugelkultur bed, sequester that carbon, and save the world!

RESOURCES

For further design ideas and inspirations, check out the works of two of the finest hugelkulturists around: the almighty, glorious Sepp Holzer; and the Duke of Perma-culture, Paul Wheaton. These guys are proving the fertility of hugelkultur beds in the extremes of the Austrian Alps and the Montana Rockies. They are truly Hugelkultur Ninjas!

- www.richsoil.com/hugelkultur/- A great hugelkultur article by Paul Wheaton
- "Sepp Holzer's Permaculture: A Practical Guide to Small-Scale, Integrative Farming and Gardening"—An awesome book by Sepp Holzer!

Fruit Wines

We generally only think of grapes when it comes to wine, but delicious wine can be made with any fruit, plus many herbs, flowers, vegetables, and even just honey alone. Grapes have taken the forefront because they have a good natural balance of sugars, tannins, and acids, but I'd take a bottle of strawberry rhubarb or persimmon wine over a grape ferment any fine drinking day.

Fruit trees and bushes can quickly overwhelm us with heavy harvests and the need to preserve. There is only so much jam one can jar up and pie one can eat when the fruit is falling. Fortunately, fruit wine—also called "country wine"—is easy to create, uses up a lot of fruit, stores well, makes great gifts, and you'll never feel like you have too much!

There is an art to winemaking—similar to gardening—that is based on balance and taste. The following recipe is a rough outline that has varying nuances depending on the fruit, herb,

or veggie you're fermenting. The blackberries in this recipe can be swapped out with any fruit at the same weight.

Note: Fermenting wine and beer is not a dangerous venture. If you steer off course in your brew, you'll just end up with vinegar or a funky sour batch that you may even like!

BLACKBERRY WINE

INGREDIENTS - MAKES 1 GALLON

- ❏ 3½ lbs blackberries
- ❏ 1 package wine yeast
- ❏ 1 teaspoon yeast nutrient
- ❏ 1½ cups orange juice at room temperature
- ❏ 5 pints (10 cups) boiling water
- ❏ 2¼ lbs sugar

1. Put blackberries in a tub of water and remove those that float to the top, as well as pieces of leaves, stems, etc. Rinse and crush up.
2. Place crushed fruit and juice in a 2-gallon slow cooker or food-grade plastic bucket. Pour boiling water over the fruit.
3. Stir in sugar until dissolved, then cool to room temperature.
4. In a small clean jar mix, together the room-temperature orange juice with wine yeast and yeast nutrient. Shake it up, and let it sit for one to two hours, until bubbly.
5. Stir the orange juice mixture vigorously into the fruit mixture.
6. Cover the bucket or crock with a clean cloth and store at 60-70 degrees.
7. Stir twice a day (every 12 hours), with a sterile spoon, for a week.
8. After 10 days siphon off juice into a one-gallon, air locked vessel
9. Store for three months, then bottle it.
10. Let it sit in the bottle at least 6 months, then enjoy—and send me some!

For more information, and to order the wine yeast, yeast nutrient, siphon, and airlock jugs, visit your local brew store, or check out www.northernbrewer.com.

Favorite books for uncommon ferments: "Making Wild Wines & Meads," by Pattie Vargas and Rich Gulling, and "Wild Fermentation," by Sandor Katz.

Earthen Ovens

There is something about fire and food that brings people together. Add pizza, and it's a party. Plus, building earthen ovens is as fun as using them—and gives you license to sling mud! Earthen ovens are made with "cob," an old English word basically meaning "lump." Cob is a free-form "earthen concrete" made with subsoil, sand, and straw. It's the American equivalent of adobe, only not fashioned into bricks but rather rolled as balls and hand-worked into form. It's easy and fun. Read on.

Earthen Ovens vs Brick Ovens

The big difference between earthen ovens and brick or stone ovens is the insulated design and ergonomic form of earthen ovens—they reduce firing time and extend baking time. The mud designs I build have 9-inch-thick walls made up of varying layers to trap heat; whereas, brick or stone allows the heat to quickly escape out of the oven. Another big plus with the earthen ovens is that you don't have to be a mason to build with mud, and you don't have to look very hard to find your materials. A truly ecological and edible landscape feature, these ovens are fashioned from local materials, usually found right under foot.

Earthen, or cob, ovens can be thrown together in a day (for short-term use) or created stoutly and thoroughly for a long life of use. The latter is the one we're going to cover here.

Basic Steps

1. Dig and build a foundation
2. Mix your mud
3. Form an insulation ring
4. Lay floor brick
5. Make a sand form

6. Put on the first mud layer
7. Cut out the door
8. Insulate & plaster
9. Fire it up!!
10. Bake, eat, and enjoy!

How Big Should Your Oven Be? Bigger Isn't Always Better!

Your cob oven is an exception to the "bigger is better" rule. Unless you plan to use your oven for large-scale production, a final interior cooking space of 22 inches is plenty. That's enough room for at least six loaves of bread, your 9 x 13-inch casserole dish, or a big ol' coconut cream pie. An oven bigger than this takes a *lot* more time, material, and wood. Even obtaining five more inches of cooking space will require you to work much harder for space you likely will never use. So, following this theory, this chapter shows how to build an oven with a finished 22-inch interior.

Location

When deciding on the site of your earthen oven, you have many things to consider — how far you'll need to carry things to and from the kitchen, the nearness to your firewood, fire hazards, and which way the smoke blows. Also the oven will need to be covered, ideally with a small roof, so look for opportunities to use protected spaces or overhangs. Recently

Materials to Scrounge

- ☐ Couple of old five-gallon buckets
- ☐ Water
- ☐ Bale of straw
- ☐ 17 full-size firebricks
- ☐ Subsoil, eight to ten (5 gallon) buckets full
- ☐ Sharp sand, four to six (5 gallon) buckets (Not smooth, rounded, or beach sand. This can be bought as builder's sand or harvested from local sources.)
- ☐ Strong tarp, approximately 8 x 8 feet
- ☐ Gravel or chunks of broken up concrete (urbanite)
- ☐ Sawdust or hamster bedding

Tools

- ☐ Pair of feet, or at least one foot
- ☐ Work boots, if you're squeamish
- ☐ Old clothes or swim suits
- ☐ Wheelbarrow
- ☐ Tape measure
- ☐ Shovel
- ☐ Scrap pieces of 2 x 4 lumber

Optional

- ☐ Bluegrass music for the "Cob Boogie"
- ☐ Strong screen mesh
- ☐ Level
- ☐ Machete
- ☐ Cow manure

I discovered a good spot in my father's open-sided shed. We kicked out his mower and built a beauty of a cob oven.

In general I try to locate ovens as close as safety allows to my kitchen, since running back and forth during the baking process is inevitable. Finally, the oven door should face away from the prevailing wind to help your fire burn better.

Swamp Monster living in the shed!

1. Dig and build a foundation
Setting the Base

Unless you are building on top of an existing concrete or asphalt foundation, half the effort of building an earthen oven is in digging the foundation and setting the base. The plus side of the excavation is that it provides the building soil you need for the oven. In northern climates, you'll want a draining foundation as deep as your local frost line to avoid frost heaving. In the Mid-Atlantic region where I'm from—USDA Zone 7—it can get down to 0 degrees, so I dig down at least 20 inches. For warmer climates—zones 8 and up—12 inches in depth is good.

For a small oven with a final 22-inch interior, I recommend a circular foundation with a 4-foot-diameter base. Start by placing a stake in the center of where the oven is to be, tie on a piece of string two feet long, and mark your circle. The uppermost layer of soil you dig out is valuable as garden soil or piling up on your hugelkultur, so place it to one side. Put the remaining deeper soil, the subsoil, on a tarp nearby, as it's probably good for the oven making. Dig down to the appropriate depth for your zone. If you're in an area that receives a fair amount of water, cut a drain out. The drain should be about two feet long, with a bowl at the end filled with rubble, as shown at left.

You should now have a hole that is 4 feet across, and between 12 and 36 inches deep, depending on your climate. You may also have a drain. The foundation and drain hole can now be filled with

Foundation excavation with drain.

well-packed gravel, stones, or urbanite (chunks of concrete).

Once you're at surface level again, there are many options for building up the base for your earthen oven. Base options are only limited by the imagination—an old dryer, set of rims, urbanite, rammed earth tires. . . . If it's wood, just make sure it has good fireproof insulation from flames, and build it out and away from the house!

I prefer to make my bases with dry stack stone, urbanite, or rammed earth bags. Earth bags are simply misprinted poly bags filled with soil and packed into large bricks. They form a nice circle that can be filled with gravel and then plastered over for an earthen look. (A great manual on earth bag building is "Earth Bag Construction" by Donald Kiffmeyer and Kaki Hunter.)

A very handsome option but a trick to pull off is using dry-stacked rock as a base (below). Using concrete or mud mortar between the rocks is fine as well. The base height can be anything from getting it just off the ground to up to 4 feet tall. I've found that the ideal base height is 36 inches from the ground. If it's for the kids to use, keep it at a shorter height.

Dry stack stone base with gravel infill.

Test bricks freshly made.

2. Mix your mud

Test Bricks

My favorite method of soil testing for the right cob mixture is making test bricks. With test bricks, you not only get to know the character of your soil, but you can also sort out the optimum soil/sand ratios for the coming oven layers.

Before we make the mix for the test bricks, let's look at the soil underfoot. If your subsoil sticks to your boots and tires when wet and gets hard and strong when dry, then you can make it work. If your soil is very sandy, shaley, or silty, you will have to look elsewhere for your building soil. The easiest option is powered fireclay from a building supply outfit. More adventurous is to hunt for it along river beds, edges of ponds, or construction sites. A super clayey soil is not needed, as a percentage of just 15 percent clay works fine. The following test will help you determine whether your soil works well for cob building.

You will make four different test bricks. Note that these particular bricks have no straw added to them. First, dig past your topsoil (the organic-rich layer) where you plan to build. Put a shovelful of the subsoil into a bucket. If your soil is rocky, be sure to sift with a screen first. Mix in enough water to make a dry, dough-like consistency, then knead it by hand. Find a scrap board or surface that will stay dry for a week or so. Dump the soil mixture onto the surface and shape into a brick approximately 1 inch thick by 4 inches wide and 10 inches long. Mark it as "soil only" or "pure."

The second test brick mix will be a 2:1 ratio of soil and sand—two parts soil and one part sand. Mix the dry soil and dry sand in a bucket before adding water, then mix the dough again as you did with the "soil only" brick. Place brick #2 on the same surface as the first one and mark it as "2:1."

Repeat this process a third time, making the mix 1:1 (one part soil to one part sand). Then make the last brick with a 1:2 mix (one part soil to two parts sand), marking both batches appropriately. Don't fret about exact measurements, just do your best to approximate the ratio for each brick.

Let the bricks dry completely; this takes at least a week.

Now for the test: Are any of the bricks cracked? Do any scratch easily? Did any of them shrink? Squeeze them hard to see if they stay hard as a rock or if they crumble. Find your favorite and write down the mix ratio for future use. If none suit you, then you will have to find a new source of subsoil, make new bricks, and test again.

ROUGH COB

Now it's time to create the material for the bottom insulation layer, a thick ring of rough cob upon which the fire bricks will sit. The rough cob mix is simply subsoil and straw. This simple cob recipe is a good first mix to work with, as it is very forgiving and allows you to become familiar with the process, while allowing much room for error.

Homemade screen propped up or held between two people.

Lay your tarp out near the oven base and building soil. I find small, strong 8 x 8 foot tarps to work best, but bigger is fine if you have extra helping hands.

If your soil has large or sharp stones over ¼ inch, start off by roughly sifting the soil with a strong screen. I fashion a homemade screen by lapping together four 2 x 4's approximately 3 feet long, and attaching a piece of ¼-inch hardware cloth with u-nails. If your soil is clean of big rocks, don't worry about screening at this stage. Go ahead and spread a wheelbarrow full of soil out on the tarp and cover liberally with a layer of straw. Give it a good spray down with water.

DANCING THE COB

Now comes the fun part - the Cob Boogie!

Take off your shoes, roll up your pants, and stomp, twist, and flip the straw and water into the soil. Stop every couple of minutes to grab a corner of the tarp and pull the mix toward you like a big mud burrito. This will keep mixing the straw and bring up the dry matter from below. Each time you flip the mix, spray with water and add straw. The trick here is to add as much straw as possible while still allowing the mud to stick together and just enough water to keep it moist.

Two common errors at this stage are: (1) putting in too much water and (2) not adding enough straw. You want just enough water to make a stiff dough, and you want the rough cobb to be super hairy with straw to the point that it is hard to pull a ball of it apart. Note: don't let the straw clump, keep it spread on in thin layers. If you do make it too wet, you can add in more soil and straw as if adding in more flour to a wet dough, or let it sit overnight to dry out a bit.

Dancing and mixing the cob.

Insulation ring in place.

A cobber's thumb poking in holes to "key in" next cob layer.

Beer bottle insulation!

3. Forming an Insulation Ring

This bottom layer of insulation is very important to keep the heat inside the oven from sinking into the mass of the oven base. Make your ring 5 inches high and 6 inches wide. Start by marking your circle to maximize the base surface. If it's already circular, then begin just an inch inside the outer edge. If square, make sure the ring touches the middle of each side. Wet down the top of your base where the ring will sit. Shape the rough cob on the tarp into softball-sized balls and splat them down with a little gusto onto the base to help it stick in really well, and around you go.

After the first layer is down, poke holes into it with a stick the circumference of your finger. This is what we call a "cobber's thumb." This will be the "key in" for the next round of balls. Again, splat the balls down with a little gusto to help them join with the ring below and work them together. Finally, put down an inch or two of the cob in the bottom of the ring to seal up the base-top.

Keep it all rough and jagged—don't try to smooth it pretty. You will be coming along later with a finish plaster that will need something rough to grab onto. Save a bucket of this mix to fill gaps later.

At this point, you should go buy a case of really good local microbrew in bottles and empty them, preferably down your gullet. These empty bottles are going to be part of your base-floor insulation; empty bottles act as a great insulator. I've found the Flying Dog varieties to work really well. (Hoping for some sponsorship.)

Once you've sobered up a bit, start puzzling the bottles into the ring's base so that they fill the space

Sawdust shavings for insulation mix.

Sawdust mixed with mud slurry for insulation mix.

best while keeping half-inch gaps between them. Then it's time to whip up a batch of insulation, which is basically sawdust in a mud slurry. This is ideally staged the day before to get a good muddy bond going. Start by breaking up the soil you dug up (if it's chunky) by smacking it with a shovel once or twice. Fill a five-gallon bucket halfway with the soil. Top it off with water, give a good stir, and let the mix sit overnight. I find one bucket is plenty for this stage.

I find sawdust with a little size to it works better than fine sawdust, which tends to get soggy. Perlite works well too, or in a pinch, a bag of cedar bedding designed for hamsters will also work. Half-fill your wheelbarrow with the sawdust; pour off most of the water left sitting on top of the mud in the bucket, dump the mud on the sawdust in the wheelbarrow, and fold together with a hoe. The goal here is to coat the sawdust thoroughly with clay, getting to a consistency that balls together like dough—not too wet or too dry.

Insulation packed around beer bottles.

Topped off and leveled with sand.

Next, pack the sawdust/clay mix all around the bottles and inside the ring, covering all but the top edges of the bottles, kind of like a mud huggie! The sawdust will eventually burn out from high temperatures and leave a honeycomb that, along with the bottles, creates great insulation. Now, the sawdust layer should be about an inch from the ring top. Fill this with sand and smooth flat. This is the bed for the floor bricks.

4. Laying the Floor Bricks

For the floor's foundation, you will want to use dense fire bricks. This is one of the few items you need to purchase for building an earthen oven, but they're not expensive—about $3 apiece—and made from natural materials. Fire bricks are commonly found at stone yards or large hardware stores. You want to purchase bricks that measure 4½ inches by 9 inches. Sometimes, you will come across thinner versions that aren't as suitable for the oven floor. Old porous red bricks can be used if you're unable to find the fire bricks, but they are softer and will not wear as well.

To start laying the bricks, first mark the center of your sand bed that you've carefully smoothed flat—as level as you can. Check out the diagram on the next page on how to lay the bricks. I often start at the front where I want my entrance, or "tongue bricks," to sit and work back from there. Be sure that you place the side bricks an equal distance from the ring's outer edge, approximately 10 inches on the sides and back, to accommodate the thickness of the coming layers of cob. Don't be surprised if it takes a time or two.

One important note: keep any chipped edges of your bricks down and "kiss" the bricks by sliding them against each other into place to keep them close as possible, then tamp lightly with the base of a hammer. Try not to shift them about too much once seated, as this will draw up sand and make gaps between the bricks.

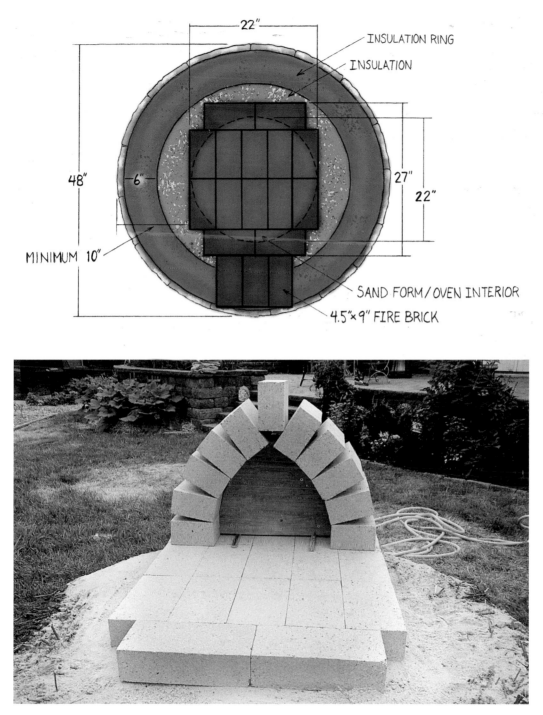

The picture here shows a built arch doorway, which has its pluses and minuses. The big plus is having a strong door entrance that can take some bumping as baking tools come in and out. The big minus is the building of it. It is a fun but challenging project to take on and may well fail if not tied in properly. Kiko Denzer covers this method in detail in his earthen oven classic "Build your own Earth Oven." I recommend starting with the simple cut-out door covered later.

Sand form

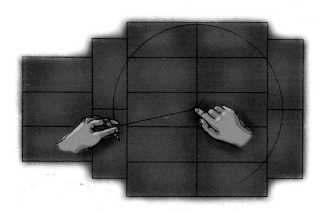

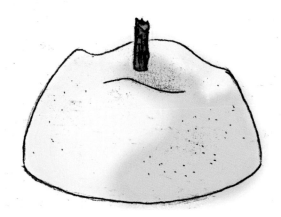

5. Creating the Sand Form

The sand dome is a solid form that the mud layers are applied to. The sand is later removed to form the hollow oven. For the sand form you want to use damp sand; I leave mine outside exposed to rain before using. Imagine trying to make a sand dome with either dry or wet sand. Forget about it.

First, tie a pencil to the end of a piece of string. Hold the string down in the center of the floor bricks with one finger. With the pencil stretched to the back edge of the bricks, draw a circle on the brick floor that maximizes the space and touches the two sides and back edge of the bricks.

It'll take about three five-gallon buckets full of sand, or about half a wheelbarrow full. Start piling and packing the sand firmly out to this mark. Try to create a vertical rise up to 4 inches tall along the outside edges in order to maximize the final interior baking space. Find a straight stick that is 16 inches long, and place it in the center of the sand. This will be your height measurement; the stick is removed once you've completed the dome. Continue building the sand up, remembering that you are shaping the look of your oven!

Once completed, the dome should be solid and hard packed. Next, lay wet sheets of newspaper over the dome. This will help when it comes time to remove the sand; you'll be able to tell where the sand ends and the cob begins.

Notes

- If the sand is a bit dry, sprinkle or spray water on slowly.
- If your sand is too wet, pile it up to drain and skim off the top.
- Rock back and forth a short piece of 2 x 4 to help shape and smooth the form. Whacking it lightly definitely makes it firm!

6. First Oven Mud Layer!

The first layer of the mud oven is like brick. Bricks are made from sand and subsoil and fired to harden. This layer is like a brick igloo with no organic matter in the mix. The mix you will use is the one you liked best from your test bricks. Note: If, by some unfortunate decision, you did not make the test bricks before you got started using the method described earlier in this chapter, go for two parts sand and one part soil.

Get the tarp back out and thoroughly dry-mix a batch of soil and sand. SLOWLY add water while dancing on the mix and rolling the tarp. Remember, you're after a firm dough. Make a lemon-sized ball of your dough, pack it hard many times, and drop it to see how it holds together. If it splats, it's too wet; if it crumbles, it needs more working and water. If it will hold form, then you know it's just right.

If you try creating this layer with the mix too wet, it will just splurge out as you pack it. I'd err on the side of dry. As soon as the mix holds together, stop adding the water. Note: sometimes your soil and sand may already have enough moisture in them to mix without water.

The "brick" layer will be 3 to 4 inches thick, covering the entire sand form. The door will be cut out later. To get the cob lob going, have someone help you by making soft ball-sized mud balls and lob them to you at the oven. If your friends have all abandoned you as a nutcase—after all, how many people do you know who are building a mud oven in their back yard?—just make up a bucket of balls first and have them on hand by the oven.

Start by wetting the base surface around the sand form where the layer will sit; this may just be sand from the bottom insulation layer. Use both hands: one to compress the balls down with your knuckles and the other to support and shape the outer edge.

First layer going up by potter extraordinaire Robert Strasser.

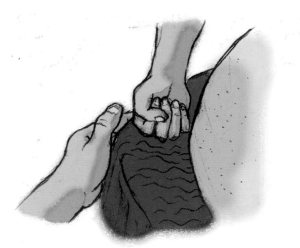

Press downward, not inward.

Finished first oven layer.

Now, the trick is to not press *into* the sand form, but rather directly down against the mud itself. Keep on keepin' on around and up, making sure the balls and layers are integrating together into a solid form. Remember your cobber's thumb to help tie the layers together. Step back along the way to see if you're shaping well and avoiding flat, high, or low spots to your dome. Use the short 2 x 4 again to help with the shape, and even whack it lightly to help with compression. If it is bulging or lopsided anywhere, simply cut it off with a machete or other large knife and throw it back in the mix.

At this point the oven should be left to dry before continuing. However, if you made your brick layer mix stiff, you could continue on at this point. If you don't have a roof up yet, cover the oven with a tarp to protect it and allow a slow cure for a few days to a week. When the cob has firmed up and you can barely dent it with your finger pressed hard, it's time to cut out the door.

Notes

- If your soil is hard and chunky coming out of the ground, soak it with water overnight to smooth it out.

- If you have a helper jacked up on caffeine and whizzing up on one side of the dome, make sure it all stays even with the other sides or it'll look lopsided.

- At the top, you'll end up packing downward some and have to guess the thickness.

- The newspaper on the dome may become dry and want to lift off; just sprinkle or spray it with water as you go up.

- If you are bulging out, then it's too wet, and the best thing is to wait for it to dry. If it's a minor bulge, I take a machete and cut/shape off the bulge.

7. Cutting Out the Door

Kiko Denzer, the guru of earthen oven building, recommends a door height of 10 inches for an oven with an interior dome height of 16 inches. This height helps maximize the draft. Begin by measuring up 10 inches from the center of your tongue bricks, and outline the arch that leads down to just inside the outer bricks. This is where those years of pumpkin carving come to fruition. I use a small machete from my Ninja arsenal, but any number of cutting tools can do the job.

Cutting out the door on bevel. The marks on the first layer are to help the next layer 'key' in.

The main trick is to bevel the cut so it angles in, making the inside a little lower than the outer edge. The bevel cut helps later if you decide to add a closing door. Smooth the edge once you've cut it; I use the back of a wet metal spoon and press the edge firmly to achieve a hard polish. The extra care you take in firming up the cut will pay back later as you bump against the entrance with your baking tools.

La Puerta (Door) *?x#!

Generally, oven doors are a pain in *el culo*. Indeed, if your only goal is to make pizza, forget about adding a closing door. I've made a variety of doors over the years and have come to accept that the best option is to brace a piece of sheet metal against the opening with a long stick. Ugly as it may be, it works great and won't burn up. Other door options can be fashioned from paired 2 x 6 inch lumber pieces cut and beveled to match the door opening and joined by a scrap that becomes the handle. Cut a piece of paper the size of the door

Easy and efficient door option.

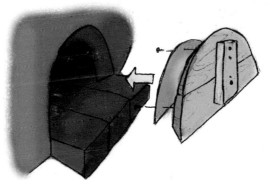

More attractive but challenging door option.

opening and trace onto the 2x6's. Bevel cut, if you can, to match the door cut you made, and screw on a piece of metal to the inside for added protection. For any gaps, just stuff in damp rags and soak your door a good half hour before using. You could even get cob ninja and make an earthen door!

8. Insulate & Plaster
Wrap in the Heat

We're now on to the second layer of the oven, which is all about insulation—holding in the heat. This layer will be just as thick as the first, although much quicker and easier (amen!)—plus, you are not a virgin cobber anymore. Just as the subfloor insulation kept heat from migrating downward, we are now going to wrap in the heat from above.

First, we want to bump out the entrance, creating a lip to hold the insulation up and away from the doorway. This lip can be made with your rough cob mix from the insulation base ring, or make up another small mix that has long, strong straw in it. Build this up around the door arch roughly 2-3 inches thick and coming out 3-4 inches. Make sure it integrates with the layer below by wetting the surface first and packing it firm. I build the lip about ½ inch back from the door cut so that when I do the final plaster, it ties in with the smoothed door-cut below.

Create a bump-out around the door frame to hold the insulation layer.

The insulation layer uses the same recipe and mix as the sawdust/mud-slip made for the subfloor. Again, remember to make up a mud-slip the night before—at least five or six buckets full. Put it on as you did the first layer, but don't worry about the consolidated packing since we're going after air pockets anyway. Be sure to wet down the first layer and join the insulation into it as best as possible. Go four inches thick, and pay attention to how it is shaping up. This is where you can even out some of the lopsided parts of the first layer and hopefully, come out with a decent shaped dome (think Michael Jordan, or, for you old timers, Yul Brynner). Scratch it all up when done, about a ¼ inch deep all around, so the final coat has something to grab on to.

Sometimes, especially during workshops where there are many hands involved, the first layer is not as strong as I like and may have sizable cracks, so I alter the insulation mix to amend for any weakness. Instead of the sawdust mud slurry, I make another batch of the rough cob, just soil and *lots* of straw, and make the second layer a dense, hairy one. This won't match the same insulation value as the sawdust but will trap heat when the straw burns out, leaving a honeycomb of air pockets. This way assures a strong structure, albeit a lot more mixing and work.

TIME TO GET PLASTERED!

The oven's final layer is when the peanut gallery finally steps up and wants to start helping—that is, until they find out you are using cow shit in the mix! No kidding.

I prefer to use fresh cow dung in my final plasters, but it is not 100 percent necessary. Cow shit has awesome qualities after going through four stomachs and comes out in fine fibers nicely glued together with enzymes. Plus it's quick and easy to collect, as compared to making your own fine fiber for the plaster. You can use horse dung, too, but I find cow to be benign in funky bacteria as long as it's been grass fed. Some manure substitutes for fiber are fine-chopped straw, which I make with some serious ninja machete whacks or a weed whacker; cattails also work when fluffy and dry. But these alternatives all pale next to good ol' cow shit!

Moving on from the shock of using manure in the plaster, let's look at the other ingredients. Plasters have a high mix of sand in them to keep

Finished plaster getting smoothed on by hand.

Good old cow poop option for really nice, smooth plaster finish.

Removing the sand form.

Time to enjoy!

down cracking. I like to fine-screen the sand with my mother's antique flour sifter, but any small screen does the job. Likewise, I fine-screen the sub-soil, giving my mom's sifter a genuine antique look! The fine-sifting makes a nice smooth plaster but is not necessary.

The ratios are:

- Three or four parts sand
- One part soil
- One-half part fine fiber
- Just enough water to mix

Dry mix the sand and soil well on the tarp, then add the manure or fiber and mix it well with a little water until it's like creamy peanut butter. Plasters can be up to 1 inch thick, but I find them usually going on about ½ inch thick. The trick in applying is to press it on firmly using the palm of your hand so that it adheres well to the insulation layer below. If it's not firmly applied, it may peel off later. If the insulation layer has dried out, wet it first before applying the plaster. Smooth the plaster with circular motions of your hands (think: "wax on, wax off").

It only takes about two buckets of finished plaster to cover the dome, but I make three, keeping the extra one for future re-plastering needs.

Viola! You're done. Now, slowly and carefully pull out the sand form, being mindful of not digging into the first cob layer. I recommend leaving the oven to harden for a few weeks to dry out before firing.

Notes: Some surface cracking is inevitable; don't let this freak you out. If the cracks go deep, then do freak out! For the surface cracks, I either live with them or periodically do a re-plaster (with the saved original in a closed bucket). To re-plaster cracks, I water down the plaster mix and dribble it into the deep cracks as best I can. I've been impressed with some ovens I've seen that are majorly cracked yet continue cooking right along.

The roof in this image is made from forest floor harvested black locust posts and a single sheet of birchwood plywood covered in aluminum.

9. Fire it up!!
Getting Baked

Firing the cob oven is an art. Having no chimney means busting out those Boy Scout or 4-H fire-building skills and keeping it au natural, meaning no fluid starters or accelerants, unless you like their flavor in your pizza.

Mighty fine pizza!

The trick is to start and maintain a small hot-burning fire. Use paper and twigs to get it going, then use split wood about three inches in diameter. What you are after here is a quick and hot fire, not one you stuff full and figure you can come back to in an hour. I tend to feed my fire about every 15 minutes, for a total firing time of 1½ hours. By the way this is great brew time; tending a fire and drinking good beer go well together.

If I'm making pizza, after 1½ hours I push the glowing coals to the side edges of the floor with a hoe, making a half-moon ring. Then I tie a rag to the end of the handle end of the hoe, dip it in water, and swab out the floor where I'm going to be sliding my pizzas. With the pizza all ready to go, I slide them in with an old French bread peel I got from an antique joint and cut down to fit my door. (Trick: put corn meal on the slider to keep the pizza from sticking.)

To turn the pizzas, I use a skinny flat-head shovel, the kind used for edging your garden, that allows me to move around inside the oven and rotate the pizza. You'll find or make the right tools; just be mindful of the door entrance and don't knock it too much. If your fire is burning as it should, your first pizzas will be out in 90 seconds. Cooking time will gradually slow as the oven cools. After a few pizzas, I throw small kindling on the coals to boost the temperature and help cook the tops of the pizza.

For bread, after 1½ hours of letting the coals burn, I take all the coals out of the oven. I pull them out with a hoe into a wheelbarrow then swab out the floor and test the heat with a scrap piece of paper to see that it's not too hot. You want the paper to take a minute to turn a deep brown; if the paper blackens quickly, then wait five minutes and try again. When it takes a minute to brown, that's your cue to pack your loaves in. I find my loaves are ready at 45 minutes. To test them, tap the bottom to hear if they have a hollow sound. As the oven temperature drops, you can use the remaining heat to make cookies, granola, roast nuts, dry fruit, mushrooms—the list is endless!

Finally, invite me over to sample your fine food and libation!

Cob Oven Pizza

The essence of a good pizza is in its sauce. And cooking down fresh tomatoes and herbs gets you that sauce.

SAUCE INGREDIENTS - MAKES 4 CUPS

- ❑ 1 tbsp. olive oil
- ❑ 3 cloves of garlic, minced
- ❑ 1 tbsp. fresh chopped oregano (1 tsp dried)
- ❑ 2 pounds diced fresh tomatoes (2 x 14.5 ounce cans, juice and all)
- ❑ 1 tsp sugar (helps cut the acidity)
- ❑ ½ tsp red pepper flakes (optional if kids don't go for hot)
- ❑ ½ tsp salt
- ❑ Black pepper to taste

PUT IT TOGETHER

1. Warm the olive oil in a medium sized pan.
2. Add in the garlic for about a minute.
3. If using dried oregano, add it now. If using fresh oregano, add it at Step #7.
4. Add the tomatoes, red pepper flakes, sugar, salt, and black pepper.
5. Stir occasionally on medium heat until boiling, then reduce to a simmer.
6. Simmer uncovered for 90 minutes.
7. If using fresh oregano, add it now.
8. You can leave your sauce chunky, or put in a blender to create a smooth sauce. NOTE: be careful when blending hot sauce; it's best to let it cool so it does not explode when blended.

TRICKS ON MAKIN' DOUGH

It seems there are as many pizza dough recipes as there are pizza makers. Some of the best I've had are simply flour, salt, and water. Any which way you mix it, make sure it is thin, about ¼ inch maximum, to help it cook quickly and evenly in the oven. Also be sure it is shaped to fit your paddle, which in turn should be shaped to fit your oven entrance. With small cob ovens this is usually just 10 inches wide. Cob oven pizzas tend to be oblong in shape rather than circular to maximize on getting through the entrance. Don't worry, they make up for their funny shapes in flavor. Sprinkle corn flour on your pizza paddle or shovel to help it slide off easily into the oven; otherwise you may end up with a calzone.

TOPPING IT UP

Add the sauce and additional toppings to your dough while it sits on the paddle. This makes for an easy slide off from the paddle into the oven when ready to bake. Many Italian pizza makers have a rule of three when it comes to toppings—limit your pizzas to no more than three flavors, which include sauce and cheese. This is the secret behind the simplicity of the Margherita pizza: crushed tomato, fresh mozzarella, basil, salt, and olive oil. Or shiitake and goat cheese with caramelized onions. The more simple the pizza, the better it will cook in the cob oven.

It's natural to want to pile on the full spectrum of toppings thinking it will be grand, but chances are it will cook unevenly. I love baking for kids who just want sauce and cheese – they whip in and out of a hot oven in 90 seconds. If your pizza is piled high, be sure to add a few small pieces of kindling on top of the coals. Doing this also helps to raise the oven's temperature after the first round of pizzas have cooked, since the oven will tend to cool and the pizzas are taking too long to finish.

Plant a pizza garden next to the oven for the freshest ingredients!

Next is building an earthen
oven on wheels . . .

VIRGINIA

09 17

753 843

MULTI-USE TAG

Shot taken at Floyd Fest along the
Blue Ridge Mountains in Floyd
Virgina. Best music festival ever.
Great for the whole family.

Acknowledgments

This has to be one of the most supported books in publishing history with over 185 supporters! Thanks to supporters via Kickstarter, an online fund-raising platform, "Edible Landscaping with a Permaculture Twist" raised all needed funds to self-publish. The creation of this book has truly been a community effort and success. This book belongs to all of you.

SPECIAL THANKS

Deb and Scott Keimig
Laurel and Jay Silvio
The Esposito Family
Bryan Voltaggio
Jonathan and Hilda Staples
Sandra J. Smith-Gill
Alice Bagwill
Betsy Tobin
Charlotte Baker-Shenk

Dan Ellis
Ellen James
Christopher Stowell
Alice Leonard
Bob Brill
Sigi Koko
Travis Tinney
Nan Rogers
Jane Kirchner
Alexis Self

Kirsten Tydings
Nicole Robinson
Sharon & Jim Lillard
Donna Pearman
Diane Brown
Geri Elizabeth Collins
Rose Ma
The Common Market

To Chris and Carolyn Judd, my dear friends and parents who have spawned and supported every path I have taken. To Jason and Jennifer, my siblings and models who lent considerable help to make me and this book presentable.

Teachers have been and are numerous, but of poignant mention are Doug Bullock, aka Cosmic Bob, the original Permaculture Ninja; Chuck Marsh, the Appalachian Mt. Man; Mike McConky and his fabulous fruits at Edible Landscaping; Chris Shanks, the plant Ninja; Jim Davis and his pawpaw patch; Dave Jacke, the edible forest garden Ninja; Sivananda Yoga Ranch's Catskills haven; Chan K'in Cuarto of Naja in the Lancandon jungle; Juan Jose, the Ninja grafter . . . .

Many thanks to Jimmy Leonard for the teamwork on many of this book's designs. Nicole Robinson for keeping the book on track and editing. Wendi Hoover for being the most patient editor. Star artist Matthew Von Herbulis for his spot-on illustrations and translations of my wild ideas into form. And Vicky Vaughn Shea for fantastic design and willingness to work with such a nutter.

And not a word would have been written without my lovely Angel of a wife, Ashley, who balanced a million things while I typed away and helped me build many of the fabulous designs herein. Te Amo Mucho.

Botany & Booze

With all the innuendos, recipes, and pictures of alcohol in the book, you may begin to wonder if I have a problem. Though I do enjoy a good drink, as do many hard-working gardeners, my focus on the spirits is rooted in preservation and making a living.

When fruit comes, it's in bucketfuls and in most cases needs preserving in short order. Juice, jams, and pies can use up a portion, but unless you plan a micro-business or have a million relatives to share with, you still have a glut of fruit. Turning it into alcohol is a "full" proof way to bring in every last fruit.

As a homestead grower on 12 acres that is mixed woodland, wetland, and food forest, I have to put together an economy that allows me to stay on the land. That takes a lot of creative thinking and careful planning. Though I grow uncommon fruits and mushrooms that have high market values, selling produce only brings in marginal income. But by turning small harvests of unique species into alcohol such as fruit wine, mead, or even non-alcoholic syrups, one can create a high dollar niche. Plus, you can count on alcohol not going out of style or losing its market, whichever way the world goes!

Cheers.

My Story

I grew up in the foothills of Appalachia, along the edge of the Washington, D.C. burbs, where back yard gardens and grape vines were common and paw paws and persimmons grew wild. But it wasn't until I was 23 and exploring the forgotten trails of southernmost Mexico that my journey of thriving and functional landscapes began.

Chan K'in Cuarto of Naja, Selva Lacandona.

There in Mexico my fertile fortunes began when I met one of the last Lancandon Mayans who lived in the last stretch of the Lacandon jungle that stretched along the border into Guatemala. The young Mayan was sick with parasites due to the shrinking habitat of his community. Through some very comical gesturing and drawings, I proposed building a compost toilet to help break the parasitic cycles and turn a problem into a resource. Agreed, we began to fashion and build the toilet from the jungle around us. As we harvested the thatch and saplings, my eyes slowly adjusted to seeing that the Mayans were managing the jungle for their food, fibers, fodder, meat, medicines, and building materials, a human-centered ecosystem. They were imitating natural patterns and cycling resources to provide for all their needs and economy.

Young Lancandon with jungle built compost toilet ready for use.

My world shifted from theory to reality, and I realized that it is possible for us to live in a regenerative way with ourselves and landscapes.

Then I got sick with typhoid, salmonella, amoebas, you name it funky bacteria and was pretty much carried out of the jungle. Fortunately for the Lacandon—but too late for me—we had completed the compost toilet and begun breaking the parasitic cycle. I returned home to the familiarity of the Appalachian mountains where I discovered permaculture.

While I healed, I sought work on natural building projects. I was invited to help build a circular straw bale community center at Earthaven permaculture community in the Smoky Mountains of North Carolina. I showed up and started stacking bales and found myself in the North American equivalent of the Mayan community. Earthaven is a 329-acre eco-village designed as a whole living system. Earthaven fashions its buildings from the forest; creates growing systems for food, fodder, fiber, medicine and craft; taps springs; catches energy with micro-hydro; holds collective meetings; and generates its own income.

I quickly saw the regenerative patterns of the Mayans in permaculture design. I was blown away to find the indigenous knowledge and ways translated so creatively into the modern world.

During this time I read news that people in the landlocked regions of Nicaragua were suffering through a drought and starving. This was shocking news to me. I had learned from the Mayans and from the practices of permaculture that this was a preventable tragedy. In investigating further what was going on there, I discovered a global pattern of land use and economy that countries like Nicaragua were pushed by debtors—the IMF and Wall Street Banks—to accept new structures of land use and cash-cropping, to maximize short-term returns. Cash cropping relies largely on annuals like rice, beans, and corn—all annuals that frequently fail and employ slash-and-burn land-use. The news of hunger was no longer shocking to me.

The combination of my learning and understanding regenerative land use led me to create Project Bona Fide, a grassroots non-profit aimed at diversifying food access. I headed to Nicaragua in May of 2001. I was 27. I think I had to be 27 to take on what I did when

I did. Armed with only a machete, idealism, and a pocket full of raised money, I ended up on Ometepe Island in southwest Nicaragua. I purchased 26 acres and began building tree nurseries and collecting fruits, nuts, edible palms, and perennial greens from around the tropical belt, to explore what grew well and could offer diverse nutrition twelve months out of the year. The land quickly regenerated with the use of permaculture design, community involvement, and a growing number of international volunteers. Today the project is thriving and offers one of the most diverse collections of plant genetics in the region, plus bilingual permaculture courses, and community-focused nutritional programs.

With the project's vision well rooted and well run, I returned home to Maryland to fund-raise for Bona Fide and translate my indigenous/permaculture skills to suburbia. I started Ecologia, Edible and Ecological Landscapes in 2010 to help flip lawns into gardens, and turn back yards into mini-orchards. I wanted to get people planting again.

The response and rewards have been huge. "Edible Landscaping with a Permaculture Twist" documents Ecologia's first three years of growing.

Life's next chapter is completing a circular straw bale home built with round wood from our land and designing a homestead that reflects the local resources. The center piece of it all is raising Ashley's and my little one—one of the next generation of permaculture Ninjas.

En Paz,
Michael Judd
August 2013
Frederick, Maryland

Bona Fide helpers.